The Medieval Garden

SYLVIA LANDSBERG

BRITISH MUSEUM PRESS

*To my parents and husband
who have given me gardens*

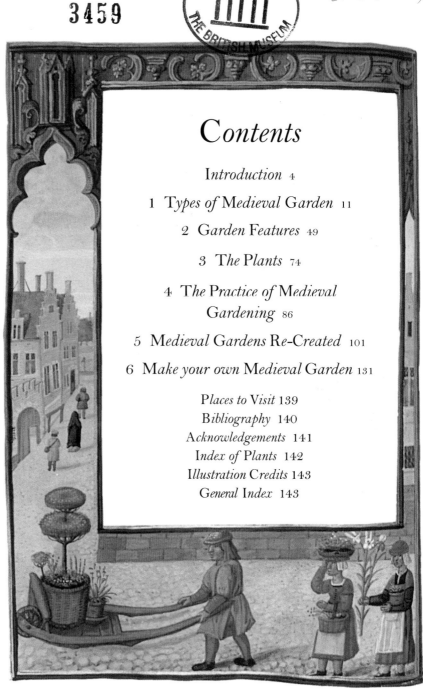

Contents

Introduction

The quest for the medieval garden is tantalising. The present sum of all our fragments of knowledge does not reveal the configuration of an actual medieval garden, other than a few Hispano-Arab ones. For visual evidence of small gardens we have to look to works of art; and for glimmerings of physical evidence of a major landscape style – of man-made water features, parks and woods, worthy of the flowering of gothic architecture – we have to look to recent archaeological studies.

Revelation of the elusive art and craft of medieval gardening is however made possible through what is termed garden 're-creation', and medieval creation and present-day re-creation are the subjects of the following pages. They are explored through an interpretative approach to existing documentary knowledge.

The story begins in Europe with Charlemagne in *c.* 800, and ends in England about 1500, by which time Renaissance features were filtering into garden design. Since gardens are viewed in the following text primarily from an English standpoint, it is not our purpose to dwell in detail on the link between medieval gardens and the major events of European history. However we should be aware of certain background influences which had a unifying effect. For instance Charlemagne in his *Capitulare de Villis*, written in about 800, stipulated the plants and estate style which should be established throughout his empire. This initially gave an agricultural and horticultural unity, tempered by climate, to leading households and also monasteries throughout much of the land which is now covered by France, Germany, Switzerland, Netherlands, Northern Italy and Austria. Another major influence originated in the Near East, as a result of the seventh-century Arab invasion of Persia. The Arabs absorbed rather than destroyed the civilised lifestyle which they had found there and brought many facets of it to Europe by invasion through southern Spain, including the release of Greek and other pharmaceutical texts by translation from Greek to Arabic, and subsequently from Arabic to Latin. In this way European medical practitioners of the period, who were trained in the new medical schools, were introduced not only to long lists of medicinal plants, but also to the concept of the garden as a place of refreshment, conducive to health through both repose and exercise. Throughout Europe and England such medical men attended royalty and the nobility ensuring dissemination of those ideas, in addition to which they were spread by scholars travelling between medical schools, botanic gardens and monasteries.

During this period the definition of nationhood was so fluid that we cannot think in terms of distinctive national garden styles, other perhaps than a Hispano-Arabic one, and although an increase in the number of garden plants has been charted, we cannot discern an evolution of style and we certainly cannot speak of a specifically English style. The latter concept is in fact largely irrelevant since England was then more closely linked with Europe than at any subsequent period, by language, politics, cultural contacts and intermarriage. Seventeen of the twenty-two medieval English queens were born abroad, and gardens were often designed for the pleasure of ladies of the court.

To re-create gardens of this era, for which only two contemporary plans exist, virtually no realistic illustrations before the late fourteenth century and barely an English one at all, we have to piece together scraps of evidence from documentary sources, art, poetry, cookery, medicine and social life, and not neglect evidence from the living countryside in which many medieval practices are perpetuated. It would still be impossible to visualise gardens of the Middle Ages, or to undertake present-day construction were it not for the classic work *Mediaeval Gardens* by John Harvey, completed in 1981, which is a by-product of over forty years of reading English building documents. Here his fundamental knowledge and insight regarding English gardens, and his appraisal of the European horticultural background, are coupled with copious illustrations and twenty-two tabulated plant lists (and more in later publications).

In reviewing the medieval literature relevant to garden construction one point soon becomes clear. Today a written work is partly a harvest garnered by the author from earlier writings and from personal observations; but, through the process of printing, it can be thought of also as seedcorn for dispersal in the minds of numerous readers, disseminating designs and existing practices, and thereby influencing the future. Medieval horticultural treatises useful for design have to be assessed regarding likely circulation. Some, of which only one copy exists, are valuable as a statement of the status quo, rather than being influential documents at the time. This does not diminish their value to us. In connection with precepts of design for instance, two continental writers of basic importance were Albertus Magnus, a widely travelled Dominican churchman of German origin, whose encyclopaedic works contained a section *De vegetabilibus et plantis*, written in about

1260, and Piero de' Crescenzi, a Bolognese lawyer in Italy who wrote *Ruralium Commodorum Liber* in 1305. Their value lies in the recording of what actually already existed on the continent, which can be corroborated by documents in England, rather than in generating subsequent designs.

For the plant component in the re-creation of English gardens the choices are straightforward, again due to John Harvey's immense work in unambiguously equating almost every medieval plant name with plants which are still available today. For English re-creations his English lists can be chronologically studied, the arguments for omission or inclusion of plants in any particular garden re-creation being viewed against the social background. Regarding both designing and planting, the most useful English documents which John Harvey has analysed have been the following: Aelfric's schoolboy vocabulary list of 995; the eleventh-century poem *Macer Floridus*, in an English version of which, written about 1395, the medical uses of plants are included; the fourteenth-century English Henry the Poet's description of his 'Square Garden', with plant lists; and the fourteenth-century translation of the classical writer, Palladius, widely read in monasteries, which incorporates useful horticultural comments. A poem of the same century by Jon Gardener, who was probably a royal gardener, contains plant lists and practical gardening details. There are also the plant lists of Friar Daniel, the fourteenth-century physician botanist, and the Fromond list of about 1525, which is classified by dietary criteria. Although it relates to a wealthy or even royal household it can be selectively used as a basis of design for different levels of society, from our knowledge of medieval food and medicine. In the same way, the post-medieval sixteenth-century works of Fitzherbert and Tusser are a valuable commentary on the past, again written from over forty years' experience, since they give the first English descriptions of many horticultural practices which had until then only been passed on by word of mouth.

For an understanding of the detailed construction of garden features, manuscript illustrations are invaluable, though mainly of continental origin and available in realistic detail only for the late fourteenth century onwards. In the following pages the medieval paintings, etchings and woodcuts are not to be thought of merely as adornment, but as vivid documentary evidence. More can be found in *Mediaeval Gardens* by John Harvey, and also *Mediaeval Gardens* by Sir Frank Crisp, valuable for many of its illustrations. The present-day designer does not slavishly measure and copy from such works of art, but instead interprets them in the light of the very same crafts which are still to be seen today in the countryside. Craftsmen are the living and often the only link with their medieval counterpart, where nothing has been recorded on paper. I have learnt not only to develop

A nobleman's herber – a Flemish illustration for the *Roman de la Rose*, *c.*1485. The lover is about to enter through a door unlocked by Idleness. As in the basic description by Albertus Magnus two hundred years earlier, one part of this garden has turf with a fountain and perimeter beds and seats, and the other contains beds of herbs, the whole lightly shaded by fruit trees.

Seats in the form of an elaborate 'exedra', U-shaped seating, which provided an area for conversing. Here it may also have been built to accommodate the dancers of the song-dance, the *Carole.* Such a document is valuable as a mental exercise for the present-day designer. French, 15th century.

extreme respect for them, but also to consider them a formative part of the evolution of a design.

The countryside is a source of further evidence of medieval gardens in the broadest sense. The 'humps and bumps' of the landscape are being explored archaeologically by organisations such as the Deserted Medieval Villages Research Group by which the outlines and development of individual crofts can be recognised. The Royal Commission on Historic Monuments has been reassessing earlier surveys of waterworks such as those at Bodiam and Stow, and terraced gardens such as Nettleham (Everson, et al., 1991); and there is an increasing interest in the subject of fishponds and associated water features (Aston, 1988). Boundaries of numerous parks have been defined, and some still contain coppices which have been managed since the thirteenth century (Rackham, 1986). There are so far no re-creations which involve such extensive features, but the knowledge to realise them does exist.

The three Rs of historical garden design are *reconstruction,* in which plans or foundations and even plant lists of a past garden exist, enabling an identical layout to be brought to life; *restoration,* where sufficient remains have survived so that the garden can be returned to its former glory; and *re-creation,* sometimes known as pastiche, in which a period garden may never have existed on the site, but where enough is known about other gardens of the time to assemble a jigsaw of the most common features. The latter is the only process at present possible for English medieval gardens. A considerable degree of licence exists in re-creation, and indeed freedom to indulge in educated leaps of imagination is part of the process, since decisions have to be made about every square inch of a garden plan. It is left to others to confirm or reject the choices made, in the light of future knowledge, or more authentically to reconstruct or restore on the basis of facts known for the site. However in the process of re-creating it is essential to guard against falling into the

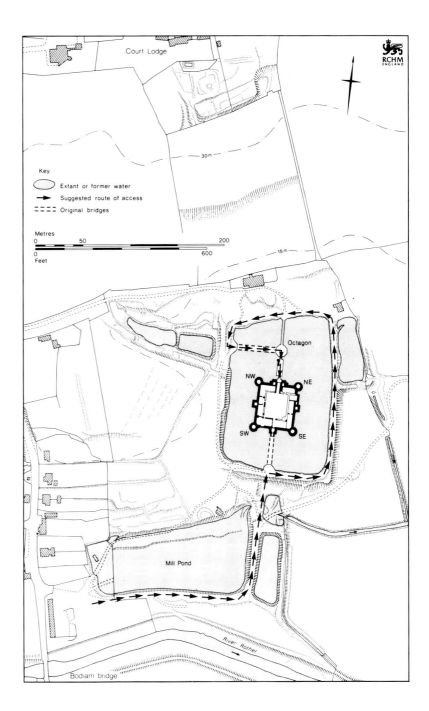

Bodiam Castle, Sussex. After a recent reassessment of earlier surveys, the castle is now believed to have been a 'show' castle as much as one fortified for defence. It was probably approached by the elaborate route from the lower ground to the south-west, from where it gradually reveals itself in its full water setting. Earthworks at a higher level to the north suggest a viewing point.

trap of merging quite distinct types of medieval garden. I myself have vicariously taken on the role of peasant, courtier, monk or queen, imagining each footstep of those who would have walked in the chosen plot several hundred years before – the bailiff's wife with hitched-up skirt treading a one-foot-wide soil path, a queen on the arm of a king requiring a four- or five-foot-wide gravelled path, and so on.

Two gardens which have been constructed in this way are to be found at The Weald and Downland Open Air Museum, at Singleton, near Chichester in Sussex. These are Hangleton, a retired peasant couple's homestead of the thirteenth century (p. 116), and Bayleaf, a wealthy yeoman's homestead of around 1500 (p. 105). They are utilitarian kitchen gardens, in comparison to two pleasure gardens: Sir Roger Vaughan's Garden, at Tretower Court, near Crickhowell, Powys, which is an example of a courtier's garden of 1450–70 around the time of the Wars of the Roses (p. 119); and Queen Eleanor's Garden, named after the two Eleanors who were the queens of Henry III and Edward I (p. 120). The latter is a typical enclosed royal castle garden of the late thirteenth century and is to be found in Winchester, behind The Great Hall, the only surviving building of Winchester Castle.

A garden which displays monastic features of the twelfth to fourteenth centuries has been re-created at the Shrewsbury Quest, in Shrewsbury, a centre associated with Brother Cadfael, the fictitious twelfth-century monk of the novels of Ellis Peters. Here, Cadfael's physic garden is of particular interest since in it are displayed virtually all the herbs which would have been available to a medical man in the twelfth century. Although post-medieval, the Tudor Garden behind the Tudor House Museum in Southampton has been included in 'Places to Visit' on p. 139, since it incorporates features and plants which were inherited from medieval times. It also demonstrates the dwindling of a medieval attitude of appreciation of gardens through all the senses, to be replaced by the introduction of features such as clipped herb knot patterns, heraldic devices, bed patterns and topiary, in which plants were manipulated by man, not for utility, but as mental conceits. In the designing of such gardens, when they are open to the public, sensitive compromises have to be made, and these and the design process are discussed in detail elsewhere (Harvey, 1988; Landsberg, 1995). But re-creations based on the three principles of authenticity, practicality and aesthetics, in that order, provide a vivid opportunity for the appreciation of medieval gardens through all our senses, which cannot be achieved through documents alone.

For historical reasons it has been important throughout the text to think in terms of imperial measurement, a system which incidentally is still preferred by most craftsmen who deal with timber. Both imperial and metric are shown on many plans, and, if it helps, the reader can bear in mind that 39.37 in = 1 metre!

1 Types of Medieval Garden

Each part full, each house in the court,
Orchard, vineyard and whitefort.
The famed hero's rabbit park …
Plough and steeds of a monarch.
And in another, even more
Vivid park, the deer pasture.
Fresh grazing land and hayfields,
And corn growing in fenced fields.
A fine mill on strong water,
A stone dovecot on a tower.
A fishpond, walled and private,
Into which you cast your net
And (no question of it) bring
To land fine pike and whiting.*
A lawn with birds for food on,
Peacocks and sprightly heron.

Poets from everywhere gather
Everyday together there ….

Lock or latch very seldom
Has been seen about his home.
No one need act as gateman,
Here are gifts for every one –
No hunger, disgrace or dearth,
Or ever thirst at Sycharth.

* The Welsh original means a
'salmon-like fish'.
From the 14th-century poem 'Sycharth'
by Iolo Goch (in Tony Conran, *Welsh Verse*).

The idea of a medieval garden immediately conjures up a picture of a small enclosed flower garden, but here, in a description of the whitewashed castle home of the fifteenth-century Welsh leader, Owain Glyndwr, the balance is redressed, emphasising the equally important elements of parks and water which would have adorned palaces and castles of king, ecclesiastic and chivalrous knight, in addition to small enclosures. Managed landscapes are as essential to our concept of medieval gardens as Launcelot 'Capability' Brown's manipulated parks, rivers and lakes are to the landscape gardens of the eighteenth century.

Moral beauty was highly valued in medieval society and one reason for moating, which was often of a non-defensive nature, could perhaps lie in Ailred of Rievaulx's twelfth-century sermon (Thompson, 1991): 'In a castle there are three things that are strong, the ditch, the wall and the keep … what is a ditch except deep ground

Leeds Castle, Kent, a favourite of many queens. The gloriet to the left was continuous with the castle until the water level was raised for defence. In medieval times there was a hunting park in the background which could be surveyed from the castle.

which is humility. The spiritual wall is chastity, and as you have this ditch of humility and wall of chastity so must we build the keep of charity.' Such ecclesiastical philosophy which was the basis also of the code of chivalry could explain both the moating and licensed crenellation of many a knight's show castle, and also of many a bishop's residence, as at Somersham Palace (Taylor, 1989).

A secular moral parallel is found in connection with yet another moated site, at Kenilworth, illustrated on p.72. A description of the reclamation of this marshy area is given in a flowery poem by the court poet Thomas Elmham, describing Lent at Kenilworth in 1414. The poem was entitled 'He built for his entertainment a pleasure garden. It was as if he foresaw the tricks of the French against his Kingdom.' And it continued: 'The King is at Kenilworth over Lent, where he considers what ought to be done. There was a fox-ridden place overgrown with briars and thorns. He removes these and cleanses the site so that wild creatures are driven off. Where it had been nasty now becomes peaceful marshland; the coarse ground is sweetened with running water and the site made nice. So the King considers how to overcome the difficulties confronting his own Kingdom. He remembers the foxy tricks of the French both in deed and in writing!' (Thompson, 1964).

Many words were used to denote gardens in the Latin, French and English vocabularies of the Middle Ages – *hortus, gardinum, herbarium, viridarium, virgultum, vergier* and the English herber; also great garden, garden, orchard, wyrtyard, vineyard, little park, and even named ones such as the King's or the Cellarer's Garden, which could imply the royal or monastic kitchen garden. We are not helped by the fact that descriptions come in documentary fragments which are often ambiguous.

A useful description of three types of pleasure garden which could be found in Italy, but which are also recognisable in northern-European documents, is given in the *Ruralium Commodorum Liber* of Piero de' Crescenzi of Bologna, already quoted. Part of his description was taken verbatim from the works of Albertus Magnus of about 1260, and this description, which is translated below, can possibly be traced back even further to the most widely read encyclopaedia of the Middle Ages, compiled by about 1240 by Bartholomew the Englishman, a Franciscan who worked in Paris and Germany (Harvey, 1981). There is much medieval English documentation to support the garden types identified by these cosmopolitan authors. These were the small ornamental garden of under an acre, known in England as a herber, containing a lawn and herbaceous borders; an orchard type of one to four acres or more, laid out in a regular manner, the function of which was to provide fruit and also shady alleys for walking beneath flowering trees of all kinds; and a third park-like type populated with animals and birds to watch, in contrast to the hunting park where the same animals were reared for slaughter.

The three types are related to different social levels. Royalty and the nobility would have had all three types, covering upwards of fifteen acres, such properties in England being commonly interwoven with moats and chains of ponds, and lying adjacent to a large hunting park of some two hundred acres. Owners of more moderate means would lay out the first and second types only, over some two to five acres, perhaps enlarging the customary ditches to make prestigious moat-like features. More humble properties, such as those of the new town bourgeoisie, or lesser manors which were rarely visited by the owner, might only have the first type of herber garden, of under an acre.

The Herber, or Small Enclosed Garden

The Albertus Magnus description copied by Crescenzi (Harvey, 1981), states that:

Care must be taken that the lawn is of such a size that about it in a square may be planted every sweet-smelling herb such as rue and sage and basil, and likewise all sorts of flowers, as violet, columbine, lily, rose, iris and the like. Between these herbs and the turf, at the edge of the lawn, set square, let there be a higher bench of turf, flowering and lovely; and somewhere in the middle provide seats .... Upon the lawn too against the heat of the sun trees should be planted or vines trained .... Shade is more sought after than fruit, so that not much trouble should be taken to dig about and manure them, for this might cause great damage to the turf ... the trees should not be bitter ones ... but with perfumed flowers and agreeable shade, like grapevines, pears, apples, pomegranates, sweet bays, cypresses and such like. Behind the lawn there may be a great diversity of medicinal and scented herbs.... There should not be any trees in the middle of the lawn, but let its surface delight in the open air .... If the midst of the lawn were to have trees planted on it spiders' webs would entangle the faces of passers by. If possible a clean fountain of water in a stone basin should be in the midst. It is delight rather than fruit that is looked for in the pleasure garden.

This thirteenth- to early fourteenth-century description of a herber gives a clue to the underlying pattern behind many later illustrations. The 'Square Garden' of

LEFT *A sophisticated herber*, including a trellised loggia, a walled area of square beds of turf or herbs, a flowery mead with arbour and a hedged garden with fountain. Beyond is a park-like landscape with river. 1490.

RIGHT *A fortified Netherlands manor house herber*. The beds, which contain topiary shrubs and trelliswork supports for pinks, also give proof of herbs neatly bedded in rows. A managed landscape can be glimpsed beyond. For further detail compare this copy of *c.*1490 with another version in Harvey, 1981, pl.VIIA.

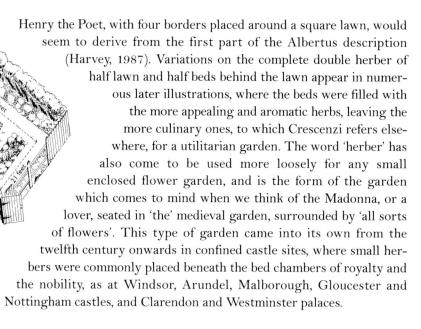

Henry the Poet, with four borders placed around a square lawn, would seem to derive from the first part of the Albertus description (Harvey, 1987). Variations on the complete double herber of half lawn and half beds behind the lawn appear in numerous later illustrations, where the beds were filled with the more appealing and aromatic herbs, leaving the more culinary ones, to which Crescenzi refers elsewhere, for a utilitarian garden. The word 'herber' has also come to be used more loosely for any small enclosed flower garden, and is the form of the garden which comes to mind when we think of the Madonna, or a lover, seated in 'the' medieval garden, surrounded by 'all sorts of flowers'. This type of garden came into its own from the twelfth century onwards in confined castle sites, where small herbers were commonly placed beneath the bed chambers of royalty and the nobility, as at Windsor, Arundel, Malborough, Gloucester and Nottingham castles, and Clarendon and Westminster palaces.

Artist's impression of a small medieval herber, based on a description by Albertus Magnus, *c.*1260. The turfed section contains ornamental flowers and aromatic herbs, the bed section contains mainly medicinal herbs. Here the triangle method of laying out is also added, using an 84-foot cord in 3:4:5 ratio (21:28:35 feet). Similar double, or two-part, herbers are implied in the illustrations on pp. 6, 54 and 85.

The Orchard

Illustrations of orchards are rare. According to Crescenzi, who was writing in Italy, they were to be bounded by a ditch and flowering hedge of hawthorn, roses and fruit trees, and the area within was to be ploughed, raked, made flat and marked out with a cord. Fruit and nut trees, such as apples, pears, mulberries, cherries, plums, figs, nuts, almonds and quinces, were to be planted. The trees were to be planted in rows, sixteen to twenty feet apart, with vines between, and the ground beneath was to be mattocked round the trunks, and new soil added, unlike the grassy herber where such disturbance would be ugly. Trellises, tunnel arbours and seat arbours of poles completed the orchard. Crescenzi also mentions that the turf was to be mowed twice a year for beauty. A late illustration of his work suggests paths at right angles, surfaced with either sand or turf. The numerous references to shady alleys and to suggestions of tunnel trellises supporting vines in English gardens could refer to both this and the herber type of garden. A poem written by James I of Scotland about 1488, when he was imprisoned at Windsor Castle, describes such a scene:

> Now there was fast made by the touris wall
> A garden fair, and in the corners set
> An arbour green with wandis long and small

A pentice, or gallery, where chess and backgammon could be played. A ball game is played in the foreground. In a restricted courtyard such perimeter cloisters or pentices provide the same shade as the perimeter trees around the Albertus lawn, which require more space. Flemish, 15th century.

Railit all about; and so with trees set close
Was all the place, and hawthorn hedges knet
That life was non walking forby
That might within scarse ony wight aspy
So thick the bewis and the leaves green
Beshaded all the alleys that there were ....

English documents reveal that orchards were surrounded by a variety of boundaries, such as the traditional ditch and quickset hedge, wattle, palisade or walls and also by moats, which were reasonably animal-proof. There are several thousand moated sites, of unknown purpose but still identifiable, scattered round the country, many of which have been said by archaeologists to have contained nothing, that is no buildings, but an orchard of some type is a real possibility (Currie, 1992). The additional purpose of the boundary, however, was legal demarcation of territory, in order to obtain maximum compensation against theft. According to an early Frankish law the minimum features of an orchard, for legal compensation, were twelve trees in an enclosure. At a spacing of sixteen to twenty feet an area of about 60 x 80 feet would be required for the smallest orchard. The poignant twelfth-century poem, referring to Henry II's war against Scotland, reveals the impossibility of preventing vandalism (Amherst, 1896):

They did not lose within, I assure you I do not lie,
As much as amounted to a silver denier.
But they lost their fields, with all their corn,
Their gardens ravaged by those bad people.
And he who could not do any more injury took it in his head
To bark apple trees – it was bad vengeance.

The largest recorded is the twelve-acre orchard at Llanthony Priory in 1199, which could have contained between 400 and 1000 trees, depending on spacing.

Detailed evidence exists for only three orchards. One is the cemetery orchard on the Swiss, ninth-century, St Gall monastery plan (p. 38); this was 60 x 125 feet and contained thirteen trees or locations for them, their arrangement dictated by being planted between the tombs of the dead monks. The site of the second orchard is in Rosamund's Bower, Everswell (p. 21), where the hundred pear trees planted by Henry III in 1268 must have been at a sixteen- to twenty-foot spacing, to fit within an area on a still-existing plan, which was not already occupied by pools and buildings. A third orchard consisted of 139 apple trees which were planted in the *curia* at Cuxham (p. 25), the trees having been ordered in four successive batches between 1298 and 1303 (Harvey, P.D.A., 1965). A hypothetical plan for the Cuxham orchard can be read into the documented facts. Apart from one extra tree, perhaps a replacement, all the tree batches were in multiples of six, suggesting a long-term plan, and this might account for two men being employed to dig up thorn for two weeks and four days, five years prior to the planting. The ground could have been fallowed in the traditional way to remove weeds and add manure, followed by planting with vetches or pulses to enrich it, the one-off planting of an acre of beans in the garden being suggestive of this. At Bury St Edmunds beans were the first choice of crop when the sacrist's house was demolished in the twelfth century (Butler, 1949). There was too little space within the Cuxham *curia* to plant as many as 139 trees at the thirty-six-to forty-foot distance recommended by later writers such as Fitzherbert, but there could have been room for twenty-foot spacing.

Orchards were valued not only for the pleasure given by blossom, scent and shade, but also for their produce. In England, as in Italy, mulberry, medlar, quince, chestnut and walnut augmented the basic apple, pear and cherry trees; sometimes a whole orchard named a *pomarium* was devoted to apples, others solely to cherries and others to nuts, as at Cuxham. Surplus cider, perry and verjuice were commonly sold, the latter being an acid, salted juice, prepared from fermented unripe apples and grapes. It was used in cook-

LEFT *A walled pleasance.* The isolated walled garden with corner towers for board games, and turfed area within, together with the main castle across the water, have their parallel in the Kenilworth Castle pleasance. Flowery turf, here possibly with periwinkle and strawberries, or with hay meadow or annual cornfield flowers, is often depicted with narrow sanded paths. The simple bridge is removable, to allow boats to pass. A felled coppice lies beyond the river. (Here the lover is allowed entry by Dame Nature into a garden which reveals a choice of lady as fleshly love, wisdom or courtly womanhood.) French, *c.*1500.

RIGHT *An orchard, showing a fruit tree and a pine tree,* perhaps grown for its nuts, with flowery mead beneath, and sanded paths at right angles. Gardeners are digging and manuring the tree roots. There is a fence with a rose behind, and a tunnel arbour with vines in the foreground, suggesting an orchard for pleasure as well as utility. 15th-century French illustration of Crescenzi's work.

ing, to give a sharp savoury flavour which has subsequently been replaced by lemons and tomatoes. The chief cooking and cider fruit were the ubiquitous Costard and Pearmain apples, and the Wardon pear, now our Black Worcester, which was grown at all levels of society. Some sixteen varieties of apples and pears were grown by the nobility by the thirteenth century, but even so Eleanor of Castile arranged for fruit and grafts of the choice Blancdurel apple to be sent from Paris to the royal garden at King's Langley in 1280, along with cherry wine and brie cheese (Harvey, 1982).

Sapling trees, from which orchards were established, were obtained by sowing nuts and stones in special beds, and later transplanted at a suitable stage. Pears and apples do not grow true to type from pips, so they were, and still are, propagated by grafting, the orchard, and grafting in particular, being one of the richest sources of medieval symbolism:

In the myddis of my gardyn
is a peyr set [pear tree]
it wele non per bern
but a per Jenet.

The fayrest mayde of this town
  preyed me
for to gryffen her a gryft [to graft a
  graft]
of myn pery tree.

When I hadde hem gryffid
alle at her wille,
the wyn and the ale
she dede in fille.

That day twelfus month,
that mayde I mette:
she seyd it was a per Robert [père
  Robert]
but non per Jenet. [pear Jennet]

A moated orchard with gate and stone and wattle walls. The trees are more tightly packed than would have been the case in reality. An avenue gives a distant view of a church. Flemish, 15th century.

Apple and pear varieties could be propagated by the gardener on the premises, but they were also obtained ready-grafted from commercial nurseries, and the fourteenth-century Cuxham accounts even record their delivery by cart.

For the general management of fruit trees, the soil was regularly scraped back from the roots, and new soil added in spring – perhaps it was the performing of this task on a large scale in a chill wind that caused the gardener's eleven-week illness at Cuxham referred to in the carefully recorded manor documents!

The Pleasure Park, or Little Park

Members of the minor gentry, such as the Pastons in the fifteenth century, might have had both herber and orchard on their manors but a king, an abbot or bishop would have an addi-

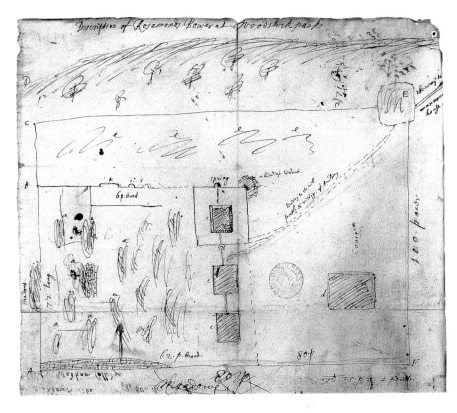

tional park-like garden, preferably walled. Here, according to Crescenzi, 'a grove of diverse trees should be planted, in which the wild creatures placed in the garden may flee and hide … hares, stags, roebucks, rabbits and the like harmless beasts may be put among the bushes'. He also mentions a timber-framed summer palace 'to which the king and queen may resort when they wish to escape from grave thoughts and refresh themselves'. Rows of trees may be planted around this building, but if in rows 'they should run from the palace to the grove but not crosswise, so that one can see easily from the palace whatever the animals do in the garden' (Calkins, 1986). Rivers and pools for both fish and wildfowl are also a feature.

The garden birds also mentioned by Crescenzi could all be found in English gardens of the park type, namely pheasants, partridges, nightingales, blackbirds, gold-finches, linnets and other singing birds. In fact, this little park has the function of a menagerie, a poetic example of which is described in a 'small enclosure' at the nunnery at Poissy (*Le Livre de Dit du Poissy*, Christine de Pisan, trans. L. Riley-Smith):

Rosamund's Bower, Woodstock, Oxfordshire, sketched by John Aubrey in the 17th century and subsequently destroyed, except for one pool, in the landscaping for Blenheim Palace. These remains of an isolated garden and building are probably as built by Henry II for his mistress 'the fair Rosamund' and contained an orchard of pear trees. The sketch notes refer to 'noble gatehouse, … a pool, … three Baths in Trayne, with water issuing from a spring, … a seat in the wall about 2 yards long'. A-F is 200 yards.

Turf bench in a park setting. The whole scene is typical of the little pleasure park of Crescenzi, with seats, and grassy launds between clumps of trees and shrubs, providing both a view of, and shelter for, wild animals. Flemish, 15th century.

There are antlered deer that run very fast
There are hares and rabbits in profusion
And two fish ponds running clear,
Well constructed, well protected with a
  strong wall
And full of fish.
And there is a plentiful supply of wild
  goats
What more can I say? I would never be
  tired, winter or summer,
Of being in that house, if God was with
  me,
It is so beautiful.

Pleasure parks gave enough space for various recreational activities. The huge park of Hesdin in northern France created by Robert of Artois in 1288 was, at 2000 acres, ten times the size of an average English deer park. It incorporated villages, and was of the same order of size as the great royal Clarendon and Woodstock Parks in England, already founded by Henry I, stocked with a menagerie of lions, leopards, lynxes, camels and porcupine. At banquets and weddings two to four hundred guests might be entertained. And entertained they were at Hesdin, by a menagerie, aviaries, fishponds, beautiful orchards, an enclosed garden named Le Petit Paradis, and facilities for tournaments. The guests were finally beckoned across a bridge by animated rope-operated monkey statues (kitted up each year with fresh badger-fur coats) to a banqueting pavilion which was set amongst pools. The monkeys and the water-operated automata, although designed by a

Banquet in a park. Grassy launds can be seen between clumps of trees radiating from a palace, so that animals have shelter, yet can also be seen. There are banquet facilities and places to sit. Note the wine cooling in the stream, and the variety of positions which can be adopted on or around a railed turf seat. Cushions protect against damp. The two bears and a lion would have been in a menagerie! German, 15th century.

Frenchman, were perhaps based on the intricate automata known from Arab writings, and bring us back to the elusive Eastern origin of the idea of the park (Van Buren, 1986).

The pleasure park has been underestimated as a form of pleasure garden in medieval England, partly due to nomenclature, partly because literary writers usually set their scenes in herbers or orchards; and partly because the documentation of park features could equally well apply to or overlap with hunting parks or woods. The typical English hunting park, however, helps us to visualise the structure of the pleasure park of Crescenzi, the location of some 1800 medieval hunting parks having now been recorded (Cantor, 1983). They averaged about 200 acres in size, with a banked perimeter to keep the deer contained. They were filled with woodland, such as blocks of coppices which provided breeding place for a wide range of animals, as well as fuel and timber; dense woodland in which deer could shelter; and tree pasture where individual pollarded trees were widely scattered, thus allowing the development of grazing pasture for deer. There were grassy treeless rides or 'launds', which radiated out in all directions from a hospitality lodge, which thus had unobstructed vision of animals of prey. There were also drinking ponds and rivers.

The little park, or pleasure park, as described by Crescenzi, is obviously a miniature form of such English hunting parks in its provision of breeding and hiding places, trees in radiating rows to allow full vision from a domestic building, and pools and rivers. Only the purpose and size were different. We know that trees in themselves gave pleasure in England, from the testimony of Gerald of Wales in his castle home of Manorbier, and at Stow Park; and the name of a wood called Beauforest is suggestive. In the anonymous English fifteenth-century poem 'The Floure and the Leafe', a day of courtly entertainment is played out in what would appear to be a park, with groves of oaks whose new pinkish leaves are unfurling, open areas of daisied turf, and small hedged herbers. We come across the name 'Little Park', which lay adjacent to the large deer park at Windsor Castle, and also the 'great' and 'little' parks at King's Langley, both of these examples perhaps distinguishing a pleasure park from a hunting one. It is tempting to think that Somersham is perhaps the first visible location of such a 'little' pleasure park, in contrast to the hunting park of several hundred acres which lay adjacent to it.

Indeed, for a possible English example of all three pleasure garden types we can look even more closely at the remains of Somersham Palace, Cambridgeshire, a residence of the bishops of Ely, which was actively used in the early fifteenth century and is illustrated opposite. Charles Taylor's investigation and cautious interpretation of the 'humps and bumps' which are all that remain of this site is one of the most exciting medieval developments in recent years (Taylor, 1989). The fan-shaped twenty-acre area could well represent a little pleasure park, revealing outlines of walks, pools and small moated enclosures. Two further symmetrical banked and ditched areas totalling about five to six acres could have been orchards or vineyards, one enclosing a chain of small ponds, perhaps for fish storage. Within a main 'moated' area of six acres some of the tiny rectangular ditched and banked enclosures could once have been

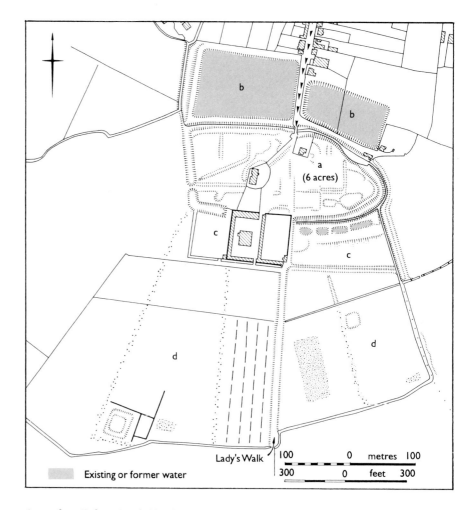

Somersham Palace, Cambridgeshire – possible medieval moated palace (a) and pleasure gardens of about 25 acres in all. Approached from the north by a causeway between impressive ponds (b), symmetrically laid-out areas (c and d) fan out from the moat and display earthworks such as causeways, banks, ditches, fishponds and a moated site.

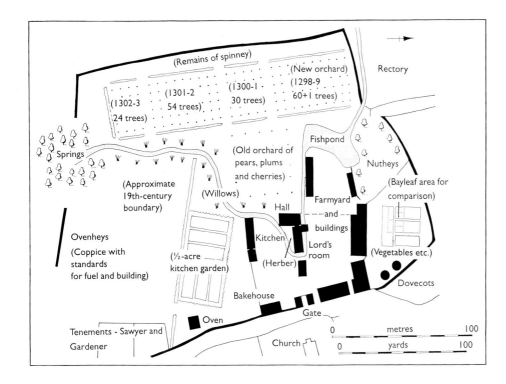

Hypothetical plan of the Cuxham manor curia in the 14th century. With an absentee owner for most of the year the ornamental part of the garden was probably rudimentary, though orchards and woods were also pleasure gardens. (From Harvey, P.D.A., 1965, with hypothetical additions in parentheses by S. Landsberg, drawn from written evidence.)

herbers of 'under an acre'.

On a smaller scale many a lesser English manor could have contained the rudiments of the three basic garden types, as has been surmised from thirteenth- to fourteenth-century documentary evidence for Cuxham, a manor and guest house of Merton College, Oxford (Harvey, P.D.A., 1965). Here, in addition to farm buildings, yard and two dovecots, the eleven-acre garden contained spinneys, coppices, river, fishpond and even deer, a rudimentary park in fact if not in name; also orchards, nutgarden and vegetable areas. A surmised plan is given left, which also incorporates a likely position for a small herber below the guest room window, to complete the scene.

Vineyards and Vines

The Romans had developed vineyards in Britain by about AD 280 as they had done also in northern Europe. After the fall of the Roman Empire wine was indispensable in the sacrament and it was often associated with the monasteries which were established following the first Christian missionaries in the sixth century. We have Bede's seventh-century testimony for vineyards, and they are mentioned in King Alfred's Laws for the tenth century.

Thirty-eight vineyards are recorded in the Domesday Survey, the largest covering fifteen acres at Bisham Abbey near Marlow. In the warmer climate of the eleventh and twelfth centuries the grape ripened well enough to make a passable wine, but verjuice made from unripe grapes was another important product which was essential for acidity in cooking and could be made even with the later deterioration in the climate. From the time of Henry II in the twelfth century English properties in Gascogny and the Bordeaux region yielded good wine. It is not surprising therefore that the number of vineyards dwindled in England, for reasons in addition to the cooler and wetter weather of the fourteenth century, and vineyards were gradually closed down, or replaced by orchards, even in monasteries such as at Peterborough and Christ Church, Canterbury.

Virtually nothing is known of grape varieties, but in 1361 a single choice Bordeaux-type vine was sent to Windsor, perhaps as a dessert grape. In particular, vines were important as shade plants grown over trellised tunnel arbours, a fact supported by frequent documents concerning English gardens (although all illustrations are continental). Froissart, when visiting Eltham in 1397, walked in the garden where it was 'very pleasant and shady for those alleys were then covered with vines' (Harvey, 1981). Vines can be branched over arbours or can be grown as single vertical stems at about three-foot intervals, as at Queen Eleanor's Garden in Winchester. Side growths from the one-foot spaced spurs give a delicate dappling of the ground in June, heavy shade by sultry August, and grapes in September. Subsequently the garden changes from a beautiful maiden to an unkempt Medusa over winter, until 'superfluities' are pruned again as described in detail by Bartholomew, the great English medieval encyclopaedist, in 1240. Apart from trees, vines were in fact the main garden shade plant until the eighteenth century.

Vineyards were not established for wine and verjuice alone, and Bartholomew mentions the further delights of the vineyard: 'A vinyerde with grene colour and merye pleseth the sight, and is likynge to smelle with swete smellynge, and fedeth the taste with swetnusse of savour, and is plesynge to touche and to handlyng with softeness and smotheness of leves, and conforteth the touche ther with' (Trevisa, 1399). At Windsor Castle in 1472, there was a 'Vineyard of Pleasour', retaining its sensual appeal when English grapes were no longer used for wine, and for the same reason the vineyard at Bury St Edmunds was enclosed in the thirteenth century 'for the solace of the monks and those that had been bled'. The monks at Christ Church, Canterbury, probably also enjoyed the vineyards outside the precinct. To improve the environment in another way a vineyard was the choice in Canterbury's twin monastery, St Augustine's Abbey. Here the abbot created a vineyard in 1320, closing off the public footpath since the area had become 'a nest of robbers, a house of filthiness and fornication, a place of brambles and bushes' (Davis, 1934).

Vineyards were surrounded by a traditional ditch, bank and thorn hedge, or more commonly on the continent, by a wall, and there are frequent bills for repairs of 'dead hedges' with cut hawthorn bushes brought in by the cartload to fill gaps. This is not a satisfactory way of keeping foxes out, which, according to Bartholomew, could be found 'lurking and loitering under leaves, gnawing covetously', and a watch tower therefore assisted in the checking of 'foxes', both human

A vineyard scene in winter, showing a lookout tower and rows of vines being pruned and tied to stakes. Note the knife held between the teeth! The ground is being dug round the roots with a pick-axe type of mattock. Flemish, *c.*1520.

and animal. The vines were laid out in rows, distances varying with the variety and method of growth, but on average likely to be about three to six feet apart in the rows themselves, with rows about five to seven feet apart, giving elbow-room for two men side by side to hoe regularly with mattocks. At such distances the 26,000 alder props brought in to support the individual vines in a vineyard owned by the Canterbury Priory, could have supplied ten acres of vineyards (McLean, 1981).

We have eleventh-century English evidence from William of Malmesbury for two methods of vine cultivation, namely bushes growing on a 'thigh' supported by a pole, and trailing on the ground. A third 'orbicular or upbounde' method (illustrated left) involving four-foot trunks was used in the Low Countries in the fifteenth century. In addition to frequent pruning of the 'superfluities' as Bartholomew calls them, the ground was kept regularly hoed in winter, the earth being pulled back to leave the plants standing 'on tip toe'.

The Kitchen or Utilitarian Garden

The kitchen or utilitarian garden, in contrast with the pleasure garden, contained food and medicinal plants as well as plants for strewing on floors, making hand waters, quelling insects and other household purposes. We need not quibble about the meaning of a herb, a vegetable or an ornamental plant, since plants were used in a multi-purpose way and there was less distinction between food and medicine in medieval times. The post-medieval idea of a complex, geometrically laid-out garden, which in the twentieth century is largely restricted to aesthetically appealing herbs, was developed through the centuries from its beginnings in the bed end of the Albertus type of herber.

The utilitarian garden was filled primarily with brassicas, usually the colewort whose nearest equivalent is a plain kale (together with cabbage at the higher social levels). Leeks and parsley were the next most common vegetable, and leafbeet and root crops such as parsnips, turnips and skirrets appeared increasingly in the later Middle Ages. Beans and peas were sometimes grown in gardens to be eaten as a green vegetable, but they were more commonly eaten dried from field crops. In addition, garlic and chives, the common bulb onion and a green-leaved one, were grown. In large institutions hemp and flax were grown in vast quantities (Harvey, 1984).

Accounts often clearly specified hyssop, parsley and sage but they usually listed 'other herbs' or 'other small plants' as a group, the range of which, however, should not be underestimated, since Thomas Tusser in the sixteenth century lists under such a heading over a hundred species for the housewife to grow. Many of these had individual medical uses, as well as being regular pottage ingredients. In the category of 'salad' plants many of the annual flowers such as borage, marigold, heartsease, langdebeef and poppy would have self-seeded endlessly, and the overall appearance of a mainly utilitarian garden in midsummer would have been one of surprising visual brightness, with a concentration of aromatic scents if a bunch were picked. The Fromond list (p. 79) identifies most of the plants which would have been grown in a utilitarian garden, in comparison to an ornamental herber.

Seed orders were often for huge quantities. For example in 1354, at the royal palace of Rotherhithe on the Thames, an order contained 20 lbs of colewort seed, enough to sow two acres, 12 lbs each of onion and leek seed, and 14 lbs of parsley seed 'for sowing in The Kings' garden in February', enough for an acre each. There was also a quantity of hyssop seed and about 20 lbs of other mixed seed, enough to sow a further two acres, making a probable total of about six acres (Harvey, 1981). One of the reasons for such vast quantities was the need to feed large numbers of guests and their retinues. Humphrey Duke of Gloucester, for example, stayed during Christmas at Bury St Edmunds monastery with a retinue of 300 in 1423, and again in 1426. He was followed by the Duke and Duchess of Bedford with 300 attendants in 1427. The vegetable gardens also served as market gardens when a surplus was grown, the produce being sold at recognised sites, and the market near St Paul's in London must have had its counterpart in many towns. Here, up to 1345, 'the gardeners of earls, barons, bishops and citizens sold their produce', but the 'scurrility, clamour and nuisance of the gardeners and their servants' had become so obnoxious to the neighbouring church that the market was moved (Amherst, 1896).

The St Gall monastery plan helps us to visualise the internal layout of medieval kitchen gardens, in the absence of any other written or illustrative documents. The vegetable garden on the plan, excluding its paths, was only about three quarters of a present-day allotment in growing area, and perhaps therefore only represented a nursery garden for seeds or seedlings, one crop to each bed. Later sixteenth-century plans reveal beds which are either parallel or orientated in sets at right angles. On the basis of accessibility described on p. 91, we can deduce that the minimum bed and path width would be four to five feet and one foot respectively. These beds could be simply paced out to any length that fitted a small domestic garden. In large institution gardens of several acres, however, for which seed and crops had to be calculated or accounted, a subdivision into 'perches' was most likely to be used, although the perch was by no means standard, and an argument for sub-divisions of an eighty-four foot line can also be made (p. 91). Certainly the perch was used to record hedging transactions, and as late as the eighteenth century the garden writer Batty Langley used the rod (i.e. perch) for crop calculations.

One way of subdividing a perch of 16½ feet is to lay out three beds of four feet in width, two intervening paths of one foot, and a two-foot-six-inch access path between one perch and the next, wide enough for barrows. Plots could be in strips of several perches in length, but one perch in width is the optimum for good access from the sides. In large gardens, where carts drawn by animals might be used for manuring and for harvesting, wider access paths of six to twelve feet would be necessary between groups of perches.

Archaeologists test their hypotheses by experimental building as at the Butser Iron Age Camp in Hampshire and the fourteenth-century village of Cosmeston, near Cardiff, and this approach has been adopted for the medieval farmstead of Bayleaf at the Weald and Downland Museum, near Chichester, where an alternative method for the subdivision of perches is given. Here, a late medieval holding has been created, of the status of a free tenant or one of the early yeomen, and the pre-cise questions which this venture raised were revealing, regarding exact layout, rotation, manuring and size (see p. 105).

CROP ROTATION IN THE KITCHEN GARDEN We can deduce that crop rota-tion was necessary, although there is no documentary evidence to explain the meth-

Joy Bulford 1990

A present-day leek bed. On the well-cultivated ground many 'weeds' can be seen which would have been used for pottage, as in the Fromond list, e.g. dandelion, borage, swinecress, red nettle, fat hen, ('orach') scarlet pimpernel, chickweed, plantain.

ods within the kitchen garden. As nowadays, most seeds were sown 'at the beginning of March or a little before', with the exception of perennials and repeat sowings. Some plants such as onions, peas, beans and the salad herbs were, and still are, harvested within six months of sowing, but others such as leeks, leaf beet and parsley can occupy the ground for twelve months or more before final harvesting. Thus, although all are spring sown, there are two types of crop, those harvested by autumn and those by spring, and this is analogous to, but the opposite of, the medieval autumn and spring sowing of field corn crops, which were all harvested in summer. There is a choice between two types of cycle. The first is a two-plot, two-year system, continuously using the ground without fertilising it, but from time to time digging up a third spare pasture plot and resting one of the others, as was sometimes done in the medieval arable system. The second type was a three-plot, three-year cycle with either a long fallow in one plot or enriching the soil with manure as an alternative, before re-sowing. This system is the one which was chosen for Bayleaf. With its threefold rotation and subdivision of plots in parallel strips the garden can be thought of as arable system in miniature which every peasant in the country would understand, from his knowledge of 'open field rotation'. It is still being perfected at Bayleaf, and we await further documentation in order to confirm it.

Arable fields were the first to benefit from dung and household refuse, but the nobility and wealthier free peasants, who had privies, had the contents dug into the garden and left for a period. Dove dung was also sprinkled on sparingly. Fallowing, as with the fields, was another method of soil enrichment which might be used in gardens, the final inedible plant remains being dug in as a green manure. Where, if not on fallow ground, did all those 'edible weeds' grow, which commonly appear in pottage lists, such as dandelions, mallow, dead nettle, sowthistles, groundsel, pimpernel, plantain, swinecress (Herb-Yve), and also langdebeef which germinates into a thick self-sown felt? It is likely that they were self-sown on vacant plots. An example of experimental crop rotation based on these principles is given on p. 110.

All the plants mentioned so far are annuals or biennials, but the kitchen garden also contained quantities of perennial plants such as savory, sage, pennyroyal, mints, violets, lovage and fennel. In some large households or institutions perennials could be grown in a separate physic garden, but for most small householders a few beds for these more permanent crops, which are best replanted every three years rather than annually, would be set aside in the kitchen garden area. The arrangement is described for Bayleaf, on p. 110. This perennial range of plants, additional to what we strictly know of as vegetables, falls outside the threefold rotation, and could account for the fourfold layout sometimes seen in later kitchen garden plans, for

Plan of the manor of Cuxham. The village, church and manor *curia* occupy a typical position at the heart of three communal fields, which are subdivided into furlongs. The plan is drawn from a map of 1767, which shows virtually the same field acreage as in Domesday and 13th-century times. The village is documented from 14th-century documents. Crops are rotated in the three fields, sown in autumn or spring, but all harvested in summer.

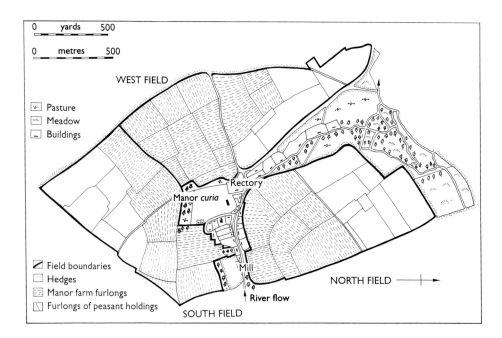

instance the plan for the seventeenth-century kitchen garden in William Lawson's *The Orchard and Garden.* Furthermore, we should not ignore the fact that some larger institutions grew flax and hemp, for which virtually nothing is at present known about the layout.

There is little documentary evidence about boundaries for the utilitarian garden, but walls, hedges with ditches, trellises or wattle, could be expected. Even within the enclosed Bayleaf garden, the kitchen garden has had to be given its own tight wattle to keep out Chaucer's Chanticleer the cock, Pertelote, and 'her seven sisters', not to mention the present-day plague of rabbits.

GARDENS IN A TUDOR PLAN OF HULL Although we have no medieval documents to help us regarding the layout of kitchen gardens, some clues can perhaps be found in this plan of Hull, which shows hedged quadrangular plots lining the town perimeter. It is now believed that the plan was drawn up around 1538, to explain the city fortifications to Henry VII (de Boer, 1973). It has many inaccuracies and the gardens have usually been dismissed as an artist's fantasy since the actual area on which the plots are drawn is known to have been built upon at the time. However it seems unlikely that the artist would draw them in such convincing variation without having seen something similar which existed in reality, even

if elsewhere. Regarding the layout of the hedged squares on the north edge of the plan (top), an initial division by crossed access paths is a common feature. Many of the resulting quarters are subdivided into three strips, some of these being further divided into parallel divisions which perhaps even represent individual beds for perennial herbs. If each strip corresponded to a row of conjoined perches, then the grouping in threes supports the idea of a threefold rotation. On this basis one could estimate the north-west square to be in the order of about half an acre including paths and hedges, more if the strips were two perches wide. Those hedged squares which are only subdivided by a crossed pathway could represent a fallow stage, grassed over as a pasture for a few years to increase fertility before being dug up to replace other squares. Squares with a few trees could represent orchards, or pasture *sub arboribus*, giving food and shade for urban milk cows. Other irregular hedged areas elsewhere on the plan could even represent land which once had a common owner, but which had gradually been rented out piecemeal for individual spade-dug allotments, as is often recorded, revealing exactly the erosion of pattern which can still occur with twentieth-century allotments.

Northern part of a plan of the walled town of Hull. Although there were no gardens in the positions shown, the design detail of the row of plots is likely to have been based on reality somewhere, rather than pure fantasy. Areas with subdivisions into plots are shown together with orchards and open squares, perhaps of meadow or pasture, all surrounded by hedges. English, early 16th century.

From the fourteenth to the sixteenth century there is documentation for the land of the original de la Pole manor which lay in the vicinity of these hedged squares and which contained several gardens of half, one, and one and a half acres, totalling some five acres; likewise the medieval White Friars' hospital garden of one and a half acres (Horrox, 1978). Far from being a fantasy, we perhaps have here the most convincing birdseye illustration we could have hoped for of details which could have been expected in reality in a cellarer's, hospitaller's or a manor kitchen garden of the Middle Ages.

IRRIGATION Although a small garden could be watered with buckets from a well or even a pig wallow supplied by water from dripping thatch eaves, there is no clear picture of the efforts made to irrigate large areas of vegetables, at least necessary at seedling and transplanting stages. There may be a much closer garden irrigation link with moats and fishponds than we yet realise, as described at Clairvaux where there was 'a garden divided up into small patches by streams flowing

between. This water serves a dual function of nurturing fish and irrigating vegetables' (Braunfels, 1972). It is possible that the furrows between the apparent
plough ridges, which sometimes appear trapped within water features as at
Alvechurch, may actually have acted as water furrows between raised spade-dug
plots. Equally if it is ever concluded for Somersham Palace that the feature of parallel strips was a medieval kitchen garden then irrigation could be a possible purpose for the furrows there. Crescenzi describes the watering between garden plots,
controlled by dams, and in my own experiment to repeat this along earth paths
between four-foot beds in my allotment, fed by a hose-pipe, friends excitedly
watched like children, reporting that they had seen such a layout as far afield as
Egypt, Turkey and the former Yugoslavia. Here in the Skopje region in the private gardens of octogenarians and in the acres of smallholdings alike, the slope of
the onion plot is so carefully graded that the water filters past each row of onions
in turn, the smallholder ready to pass the time of day nonchalantly closing one
miniature earth bank and breaking open another with his stick, just as many a
medieval gardener must have done.

Monastery Gardens

There is sufficient evidence from monastic documents to tell us that within an
English monastery could be found gardens not only for privacy, study and con-
templation, but also for recreation and refreshment, for the production of food,
medicines and ornamentation, and as a burial place for the dead – in fact all the
types of garden mentioned in previous pages. However, except for the cloister
garth, no gardens have fully survived the desecrations of the Reformation when
even a monk's topiary plants were destroyed.

A hermit-style monastic tradition was established within two centuries of
Christianity itself, but it was St Benedict who initiated the self-sufficient and cor-
porate monastic life, based on his *Rule* which was perfected during the seventh century. Here St Benedict specifically refers to Christ's words: 'I was a stranger, and ye
took me in ... I was sick, and ye visited me ' (Matthew XXV, 35, 36). With an
emphasis on warm hospitality for travellers at all levels of society and respect for
the sick, this philosophy shaped several types of monastic garden: the infirmary
and the orchard cemetery, the guest house garden, and the cellarer's garden, whose
produce catered for visitors who more than doubled the number of mouths to be
fed and housed. The contribution of monasteries to horticulture was enormous in
developing an understanding of techniques such as soil enrichment, marling, land
reclamation and drainage. Monasteries were in the forefront of water and woodland management, of the cultivation of vineyards, orchards, and pleasure gardens,

Christ Church, Canterbury. The plan of
Prior Wibert's waterworks, *c.*1165, in
which several gardens are also
shown, in particular the herbarium.

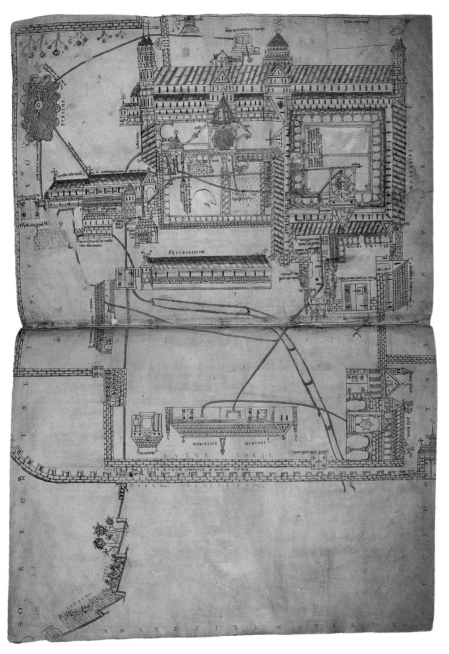

and the dissemination of medical and botanical knowledge through the collecting, copying and illustrating of manuscripts. Many abbots had a thorough medical knowledge.

The order of the Cistercian or White Monks left its mark predominantly on agriculture, pushing back the borders of habitable land, and many of the smaller houses of the Augustinians were closely involved in tending the sick. However, records of the original monastic family, the Benedictines or Black Monks, yield some of the most useful garden information. A fundamental document is the remarkable plan drawn up in about 1165 primarily to display Prior Wibert's new water system for the Priory of Christ Church, Canterbury. This is a useful prototype (although the layout of other monasteries would vary considerably in size and detail). The plan includes several gardens which are referred to here, the positions of which can still be seen today, although much of the architecture has changed.

THE CLOISTER GARTH The cloister garth lay at the heart of a monastery, always alongside the church. It was a lawn round which the monks processed at regular intervals, day and night, and they also studied there on most days of their lives. There is no evidence from any medieval English monastic records of the cloister garth being planted with anything other than turf and occasion-

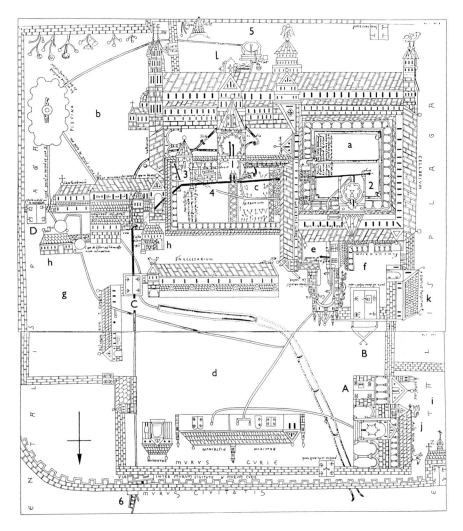

The precinct area of the Wibert plan of Christ Church as redrawn by R. Willis: (a) cloister garth, (b) cemetery orchard, (c) herb garden, (d) Green Court, (e) kitchen court, (f) cellarer's court and vine, (g) probable prior's gardens, (h) old and new prior's lodgings, (i) almonry yard, (j) New Hall, (k) hospice, (l) lay cemetery; (1) water tower, (2) cloister wash-place, (3) infirmary wash-place, (4) well, (5) lay well, (6) entry of water; (A) outer precinct or main gate, (B) inner precinct gate, (C) prior's gate, (D) inner cemetery gate.

ally a symbolic pine or juniper. There might be crossed paths, and always water in the form of a fountain or washing place, not necessarily centrally placed, with the garth at Christ Church being additionally crossed and edged by channels which collected rainwater from the cloister gutters. Christine de Pisan mentions that the grass at the nunnery of Poissy was kept short and green and never allowed to go brown like uncut hay. The colour green was in fact the key, not only as a metaphysical symbol both of rebirth and everlasting life, according to Hugh of St Victor, but also for a psychological reason. Hugh of Fouilloy said: 'The green turf which is in the middle of the material cloister refreshes encloistered eyes and their desire to study returns. It is truly the nature of the colour green that it nourishes the eyes and preserves their vision'. William of Auvergne attributed its tranquilising nature to its physical effect, being 'half way between black which dilates the eye and white which contracts it' (Eco, 1986).

THE CEMETERY ORCHARD The cemetery was another garden intended to refresh the senses of the living. Such a cemetery symbolised Paradise and was portrayed by the early Persians as an orchard, a concept also adopted throughout much of the Islamic world and southern medieval Europe. It appears in the Christian world as early as the ninth century in the St Gall plan, and it is implied in Prior Wibert's plan by the flowering trees drawn on the cemetery perimeter. The earliest English description of an aesthetically pleasing garden refers to a monastery, where the chronicler states that Brithnod, Abbot of Ely in AD 970, was 'skilled in planting gardens and orchards around the Church … and they added much to the commodiousness and beauty of the place' (McLean, 1981).

From our scant knowledge of orchard trees we could expect a regular layout in the orchard cemetery with grass or sanded paths probably on a grid pattern, and even rose and vine trellises. Both the paths, and the turf mown as hay, could yield many of the flowers which illustrated the borders of medieval manuscripts, as well as medicinal turf plants. For instance, at the Dissolution of Christ Church the area adjacent to the infirmary was called the Gymnewes, or 'mallows', this plant being known to be used as a poultice for the monks after blood-letting. Cemeteries were under the care of the sacrist, who might have incorporated further plants necessary for religious festivals, such as lilies, roses, yew (palm) and bay. In the cemetery of the Wibert plan the handsome *piscina* would have given pleasure, as well as being a *servatorium*, or storage pond, for prestigious fish, and even a source of aquatic medicinal herbs. Perhaps here it had an extra symbolism, a parallel to the thirteen trees of St Gall which may have represented Christ and the apostles, planted in rows between the tombs. The *piscina* has twelve bays. Could these relate to the twelve apostles, with the pond as a Lake Galilee, and the central fountain representing Christ walking on the water?

The tenth-century poet monk, Walahfrid, described a remembered monastic orchard of his novitiate childhood in the dedication of his poem *De Cultura Hortulorum* (trans. Payne, 1966):

> This small gift … is offered to you Father Grimald ….
> I can picture you sitting there in the green enclosure of your garden
> Under apples which hang in the shade of lofty foliage,
> Where the peach-tree turns its leaves this way and that
> In and out of the sun, and the boys at play,
> Your happy band of pupils, gather for you
> Fruits white with tender down and stretch
> Their hands to grasp the huge apples ….

However, the lusts of the adult flesh had to be kept at bay in the cemetery, for here was the only place of secret corners. The 'incontinence' of monks was often noted in ecclesiastical inspections, with firm instructions to lock the inner cemetery door overnight from Vespers to Prime, but with regard to nuns the subject was

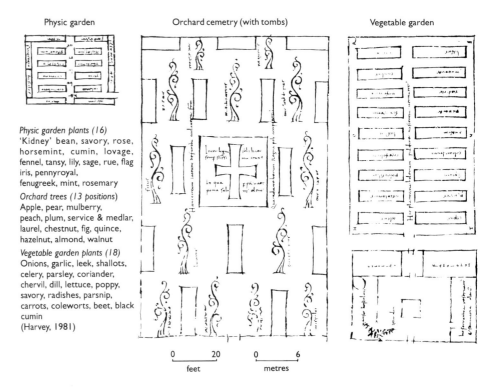

Part of the St Gall Monastery plan,
c.816-20. This plan from St Gall,
which shows an idealised monastery,
was drawn in red ink and measures
44 x 30½ in.

Physic garden   Orchard cemetry (with tombs)   Vegetable garden

Physic garden plants (16)
'Kidney' bean, savory, rose,
horsemint, cumin, lovage,
fennel, tansy, lily, sage, rue, flag
iris, pennyroyal,
fenugreek, mint, rosemary

Orchard trees (13 positions)
Apple, pear, mulberry,
peach, plum, service & medlar,
laurel, chestnut, fig, quince,
hazelnut, almond, walnut

Vegetable garden plants (18)
Onions, garlic, leek, shallots,
celery, parsley, coriander,
chervil, dill, lettuce, poppy,
savory, radishes, parsnip,
carrots, coleworts, beet, black
cumin
(Harvey, 1981)

```
0        20      0        6
    feet             metres
```

skirted round in more delicate terms. In the thirteenth century the Archbishop of
Canterbury on a visitation to Romsey Abbey instructed the abbess to build a new
garden gate *'in loco non suspecto'.* He wrote (Liveing, 1906):

In a Lily garden the Bridegroom is filled with delight and finds pleasure in gathering lilies
above all flowers. It is therefore needful to enclose this garden by the defence of shrewd and
sharp disciplines … lest an entrance be opened to any sower of mischief. This lily we
believe to be the ornament of virginal purity, which by reason of certain matters, found in
our visitation lately, we desire to protect.

THE INFIRMARY GARDEN   The infirmarer was virtually a nursing-home
administrator, employing gardeners, bringing in a physician from the town and
using apothecary prescriptions when treatment required more than his own pallia-
tive remedies. God was considered the supreme physician. Instructions for infirmary servants at Barnwell Priory were: 'go to the town apothecary and get medicines, and collect the garden herbs for decoctions, and under physician's orders,
make tisanes'. In addition to the day-to-day care of patients with general ailments,
the infirmary was a rest home for retired monks with incurable diseases of old age.

It was also a convalescent home for monks who were bled about six times a year, resulting in a continuous stream of patients (p. 84). Blood-letting was viewed as a way of relieving the stress brought on by tedium and it involved, after each episode, sojourn in the infirmary with a week of nourishing food, refreshment of the senses in pleasant surroundings, and exercise, in accordance with the precepts of Avicenna, a tenth-century Arab physician who was subsequently a great European influence.

All these needs were catered for by the features included in the large infirmary garden of just under two acres at Westminster Abbey such as a wattle bench round a tree bole, ponds with fish and even archery butts. Westminster documents further add to the vivid picture with mention of vegetable areas, staked vines, sanded paths, a dove house and a little garden, kept locked and therefore perhaps containing poisonous plants (Harvey, 1992). Harvey also tabulates nine lists of plants, mainly of the fourteenth century, giving a good idea of the plants most likely to be found in full-scale infirmary gardens, including a pottage list of 106 plants compiled by the royal physician, John Bray. A fourteenth-century description of Clairvaux Abbey reveals the pleasure which pools gave: 'Here also a beautiful spectacle is given to the infirm brethren. While they sit upon the green margin of the huge basin they see the little fishes playing under the water and representing a military encounter by swimming to meet each other'. The cemetery orchard was also a place of relaxation, as well as a harsh reminder of the grave, and in the Wibert plan it is situated close to the infirmary.

On the Wibert plan the Christ Church infirmary garden appears as a small cloister garth, and a herbarium, which is represented as a tightly fenced area. On the west side of the herbarium, the inclusion of an arched gate in the trellised fence suggests that the garden is private, perhaps even locked, and this fence separates the garden from a four-gabled building of several rooms, with an entrance to the monks' parlour. Perhaps here in the shade and the breeze invalid monks could savour the garden aromas and also communicate with monks in the adjacent parlour. (There is an ironwork conversation grill shown on the cloister side of the parlour, the word 'parlour' developing from *parler*, 'to talk'.) Perhaps herbs would have been hung here to dry, and tools could be stored. On the east side a diamond pattern trellis, commonly thought of as a fence, is just as likely from its portrayed size to be a stylised pergola. It shows side beams, and such criss-crosses are often a designer's shorthand for a tunnel archway even today. Perhaps it was a shady vine walk, thereby completing a little neighbouring cloister garth for the infirmary which would provide a dry walk in the rain. In many monasteries the infirmary area was arranged as a miniature monastery, with its own kitchens and chapel, and also a little cloister garth, as at Waverley Abbey (Coppack, 1990, fig.47).

What would the herbarium which has just been outlined have contained? Allowing for squaring off, this garden actually measured about 30 x 50 feet (Willis, 1868, fig.2). Seven east-west rows of mixed coloured plants are shown in the original plan. If, for want of other evidence, we take these rows as meaningful, then we could visualise seven parallel beds. Long beds such as these, about four or five feet wide, alternating with sand or grass paths, would fit in neatly, leaving space for access to the priory water pipes. One might expect an eight-foot wide arbour and perimeter borders and paths of at least three feet each, allowing barrow space, thus leaving bed lengths of about ten feet. The importance of this tiny herbarium plan, of only a few square inches, and the attempt to draw as much information as possible out of it, reveals how little visual evidence we have concerning gardens of the Middle Ages. The choice of plants would depend upon the purpose of this herbarium, where the emphasis could be on general medicinal plants, those poisonous ones specifically used as narcotics, those specifically related to blood-letting needs, or those particularly aromatic herbs and attractive herbaceous plants which would refresh patients by their beauty. The re-creation of Brother Cadfael's physic garden at the Shrewsbury Quest (p. 101) has given us some insight, where, on a similar-sized plot of land, there is only room for one specimen of each of the twelfth-century medicinal plants. This would be inadequate for treating all monastery patients, and points us in the direction of the small Wibert herbarium most likely being restricted to the poisonous narcotics such as mandrake, hemlock, henbane and opium poppy.

THE GREEN COURT (*CURIA*) On the northern half of the Christ Church precinct, as depicted on the Wibert plan, lay the Green Court of about one and a half acres, equal to the Outer or Great Court of some monasteries. This was virtually a village green with the bakery, granary, fish house and brewery, not to mention butcher and candlestick maker. It was the equivalent also of a present-day car park since it was well-known that it was cheaper to keep a visitor's horse at grass rather than at stall. Nunneries sometimes specified that there should be no visitors' horses tethered after nightfall. The area here was probably covered by pasture, with shade trees and drinking troughs. All visitors entered this court via the main, outer precinct gate, the poorer ones climbing the magnificent staircase, which still stands today, to the New Hall. Visiting officials and those of medium standing would pass into the cellarer's court, viewing the large vine which grew up the kitchen wall as depicted, in its traditional entrance position. These guests would be put up in the hospice, the guest master in many other monasteries having a garden for their recreation. The prior's guests would ride their horses through the prior's gate to one of his two lodgings, the old one with its trellised porch perhaps also bearing a symbolic vine. Here a tower was added later, with windows over the Green Court.

OBEDIENTIARY GARDENS   Leading monastery officials or obedientiaries had their own private gardens, and both of the prior's houses in the Christ Church plan had space for such beside them, these residences being the equivalent of an abbot's at another monastery, since Canterbury had an archbishop at the head. Abbots were the social equal of barons so these gardens would have all the quality of a nobleman's herber, and at simplest these might resemble the description of Albertus. Abbots and priors of course had other residences outside their monastery with notable gardens, such as La Neyte near Westminster Abbey, and Silkstead near St Swithun's Priory, Winchester. From other monasteries we know that sacrists, almoners, guest masters, cellarers and even the door porter had gardens, although these were not necessarily private. The sacrist had to arrange supplies of flowers for church festivals, some perhaps from his own garden, others from the cemetery orchard, just as similar gardens served parish churches. Plants would include bay, holly and ivy at Christmas, yew and catkined hazel to be carried as 'palm' at Easter, birch boughs in May, red roses and sweet-woodruff for chaplets and garlands at Corpus Christi in June, and white lilies and red roses for the feasts of martyrs. Almoners, who were daily responsible for the crowds of poor in the outer yard, probably grew mainly coleworts, if they could not order them from the cellarer, to add to the bean pottage and left over alms from the refectory table. The almonry yards both at Christ Church and at the neighbouring St Augustine's Abbey had a mulberry tree, a symbol of Christ's crucifixion.

In the Wibert plan the passage windows of the kitchen court are carefully labelled, translated as follows: 'windows where the portions are served out' and 'window through which the platters are tossed out for washing'. The dishes were probably rinsed here too, at the standpipe, visible on the plan, after being scraped out for the nearby poultry which awaited slaughter for the next meal. The trellis-work illustrated in the plan could be a vine tunnel, giving shady relief from the hot kitchen, or a trellised fence to restrict the poultry.

BEYOND THE MONASTERY WALL   The Christ Church monastery tentacles spread into Oxfordshire and as far as Kent and Devonshire, and along the roads from these outlying estates came the corn and dried fish. Nearer manors which were run by lay servants would produce animals, poultry, pigeons and eggs, all collected at the home farm, or 'Barton'; and four miles away was Caldecote, one of sev-

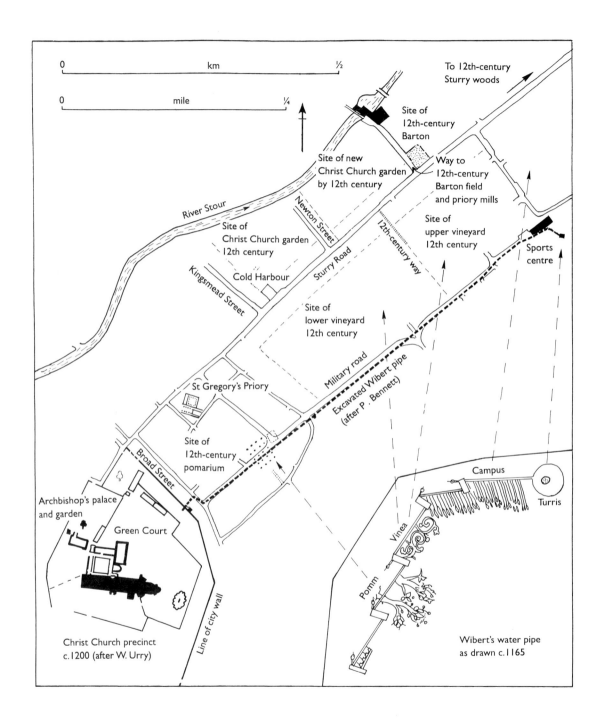

0   km   ½

0   mile   ¼

To 12th-century Sturry woods

Site of 12th-century Barton

Site of new Christ Church garden by 12th century

Way to 12th-century Barton field and priory mills

River Stour

Newton Street

Site of Christ Church garden 12th century

Site of upper vineyard 12th century

12th-century way

Sturry Road

Sports centre

Cold Harbour

Kingsmead Street

Site of lower vineyard 12th century

Military road

Excavated Wibert pipe (after P. Bennett)

St Gregory's Priory

Site of 12th-century pomarium

Broad Street

Campus

Turris

Archbishop's palace and garden

Green Court

Vinea

Pomm

Christ Church precinct c.1200 (after W. Urry)

Line of city wall

Wibert's water pipe as drawn c.1165

Plan of the Christ Church precinct surroundings, showing the positions of the Wibert waterpipe (as excavated by the Canterbury Archaeological Trust), Barton 'farmyard', orchards, vineyards and gardens lying outside the monastery wall in medieval times. The relation to present-day roads and to Wibert's sketch of *c.*1165 can be seen.

eral holiday retreats for monks. Fuel was a daily necessity and was brought by the cartload from coppiced woods at Sturry a mile away. A similar wood at Beaulieu Abbey, in Hampshire, which had been left uncoppiced for twenty years yielded logs to heat the kitchen and brewery cauldrons, charcoal to roast meat on spits, and long bundles of hazel rods or bavins which daily heated the long bread ovens, a crop of 40,000 bundles per acre (Rackham, 1986).

Water as well as food and fuel was essential, and in 1165 Prior Wibert installed his new water supply at Canterbury. Archaeological work has revealed that the waterpipe still lies beside Military Road, and from a recently identified collecting house three-quarters of a mile away one can walk down this road knowing that fifteen inches below the surface the three-inch lead pipe could still deliver water to the precinct until 1989. The gentle slope of the road gives the feel of the unhurried flow beneath land which is now encrusted by buildings, but which was once fields, orchards and vineyards. Some details of Wibert's elegant shorthand sketch have been confirmed by later research.

If there was no space within the precinct then orchards, vineyards, and extensive fishponds were often laid out adjacent to it. Forty-three acres of such grounds at Malmesbury Abbey were created for the monks to walk in, as no doubt they did in the Christ Church Canterbury vineyards. Many abbots and priors laid out similar grounds for retreats, such as the beautiful Durham Priory retreat at Finchale, sheltered in the curved arm of the River Wear. A most notable contribution to medieval garden style were the water gardens of many abbots, referred to later, and particularly that made by Abbot Godfrey in 1302 at Peterborough Abbey totalling some six acres including 'a beautiful herber' (Harvey, 1981, p.85).

THE CELLARER'S GARDEN Several acres were required for supplying the monastery with vegetables and herbs; utilitarian plants such as hay for latrines and the refectory floor; and rushes, mints and meadowsweet for strewing. Such a garden was not only for the monks but also for the numerous lay workers who more than doubled the number of mouths to feed, not to mention large numbers of visitors, and the poor.

The cellarer's garden best known to us was Covent Garden, one of the gardens of Westminster Abbey, and even until recently the name has been associated with vegetables and flowers. In many monasteries there was space within the precinct wall for the vegetable garden, probably at Peterborough and certainly at St Augustine's, Canterbury. Here the garden position has been verified by the documented route of an unpopular monk official who once beat a hasty retreat by ladder over the wall! At the Cistercian Beaulieu monastery the precinct, or 'curtilage', con-

Making a straw skep

tained beans, leeks, onions and fruit trees with pasture *sub arboribus* (Hockey, 1975). The cramped precinct of Christ Church could not contain such gardens, so they may have been sited alongside the River Stour where there were two twelfth-century monastery gardens and where a nursery still survived until the 1960s. One can even now walk along the riverside and watch allotment holders dig fat leeks from the rich black earth which perhaps nurtured the leeks of monks over 800 years ago.

One could expect a cellarer's garden to look like the northern gardens on the Hull plan (see p. 33). In addition to hedged vegetable plots there might be pasture for milk cows under scattered shading fruit trees, and fenced areas of hay, which would also provide winter grazing. Since the latter would be pleasant to walk in there might even be broad paths.

The cellarer was also responsible for providing honey for the infirmarer and wax, which was more important, for the cathedral and chapel candles, where pure scent was required rather than the putrid odour of tallow candles. Bees may have been kept in monastic orchards, but at Beaulieu in Hampshire there were thirteen wax collection centres in the neighbourhood, perhaps organised as a cottage industry, and the Beaulieu market cross was called the Honey Cross.

Peasant Closes

The gardens already described do not include the homesteads of ninety per cent of the population – the unfree peasant or true 'housebondman' on whom the manorial system was dependent and from whom the Church drew its main revenue.

We have neither a single illustration nor a single recorded word of a peasant's thought but from archaeology we know that they lived in clearly defined homesteads. On well-drained chalky or sandy regions, such as at Wharram Percy and Hangleton village, the holdings were bounded by low flint and earth banks, ditches, scarps or stockades. But particularly in poorly drained areas on clay the closes were defined by water-filled ditches with banks which would have been topped by dead or hawthorn hedges. It is these boundaries of parallel narrow holdings which have revealed the plan of some hundreds of deserted villages. Where there were ditches between the neighbouring closes and where the rutted roadway fronting and backing the properties was sunk as much as three to six feet, many closes commonly gave the appearance of separated platforms, into which it would be difficult to see.

It is a sad fact that our picture of the contents of unfree peasant closes is obtained largely from details of deaths and taxes. In *The Ties that Bound*, where the peasant is given such a human face, we learn from Coroners' Rolls that children

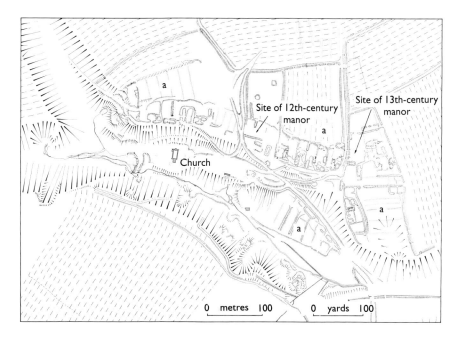

The deserted medieval village of Wharram Percy, East Riding, as mapped from earthworks and aerial photography, showing rows of peasant buildings and closes (a), track-ways and surrounding open field strips.

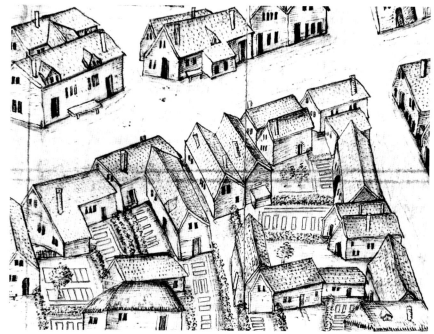

Part of a plan of Paignton, c.1565, showing unique details of artisans' gardens. Each property is bounded by a building or thorn hedge and has its own entrance. In the garden to the left two plots are shown, subdivided into parallel beds, perhaps for annual vegetables. Other gardens show individual beds, interpreted as about 4–5ft wide. These are probably raised since they are shown as separated, and are more likely to contain perennial herbs.

gathered fruit and nuts in closes, they drowned whilst chasing ducks or pole-vaulting ditches; women picked watercress from the ditches and other herbs from the banks, and washed clothes; washing anchored on hawthorn hedges was stolen overnight. From a midden heap in a courtyard a young future foot-soldier shot his sister with an arrow. Toddlers drowned in numerous pits which had been dug for marl or as a pig-wallow. In a group, arguing at a meal round a trestle table in the garden, one man struck the table top with such force it hit him on the head; an elderly man sensing his end went and sat under his tree, leaning against the trunk, to die. On 29 May 1270 Cicely, aged 2½, went into the yard. 'A small pig came and tried to take bread from her hand. She fell into a ditch and was drowned' (Hanawalt, 1986).

Regarding tax details one of the most useful documents is a remarkably detailed tithe list drawn up for the newly ordained churches of St. Augustine's Abbey in Kent in the thirteenth century (Davis, 1934). Apart from the produce from the peasant animals, the vicarages received tithes from 'curtilages dug with the foot on which dwellings stand'. Such an understanding of spade-dug rather than ploughed ground as defining a garden is repeated by sixteenth and seventeenth-century writers. The tithed animals were 'lambs, chickens, calves, sucking pigs, geese, ducks, hens, doves, bees'. The adult animals which would also be in the closes were not taxed here but we know from Cuxham, for instance, that the average peasant would have a plough horse or an ox, a cow, a pig, and sometimes a few sheep. Regarding plants, the list continued: 'herbage (pasture) hay, sheaves arising from gardens, vegetables, vetches, hemp, flax, apples, pears, and other fruits in gardens and orchards'. The meticulous tax inspector would even spot 'young timber', probably implying pollard or coppice wood of ash, willow or hazel, such as would be growing at intervals in the boundary hedges.

It is commonly assumed that the long croft areas of 30-60 feet in width which extended 200-600 feet behind the building tofts would be mainly pasture or hay, or if not, that they would be ploughed. However where crops of hemp and flax were grown, or vetches, of which both the seed and the green and dry haulms were useful fodder, they would require a considerable area; legumes filled the closes in Alciston in Sussex. Even the largest croft of two-thirds of an acre at Wharram could have been 'dug by foot' in eight days, according to William Cobbett's estimates for the nineteenth-century cottager.

This then is the picture we have of peasant homesteads. The close was in fact a miniature utilitarian farmstead with a yard separated from a kitchen garden area, perhaps an area of pasture and probably having a turf-banked corner to sit in, but little in the way of an ornamental garden. It takes the genius of Chaucer to add

Wilton, Wiltshire, c.1565. Rare detail is shown here, which would have been typical of towns and villages of a hundred years earlier also. In the gardens can be seen vegetable plots, orchards, thorn hedges, various types of paling and courtyard farmsteads. In the lower centre is a pound for stray animals. English, 16th century.

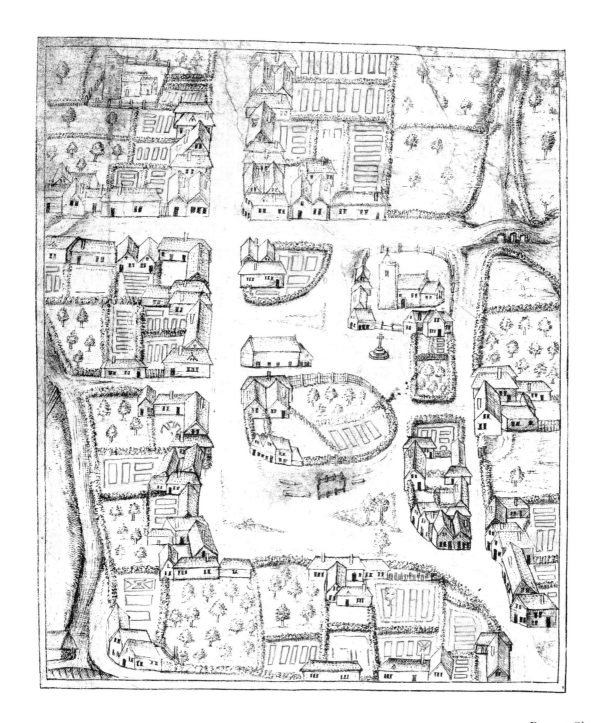

sound and movement to so few dry facts, as in his description of the poor widowed dairywoman in her dry-ditch and stick-fenced garden. Here on a sunny day stood Chanticleer the cock (*Nun's Priest's Tale*):

> And so befel that, as he caste his eye
> Among the worts* on a butterfly,
> He was aware this fox that lay full low ....
> [The fox then jumped and caught the cock.]
> The silly widow and her daughters two
> Herd these hens cry and maken woe
> And out of doors started they anon.
> And saw the fox towards the grove gone
> And bear upon his back the cock away
> And cried 'Out', 'Harrow' and 'Weylaway'
> 'Ha-ha the fox' and after him they ran ....
> Ran Colle our dog and Talbot and Gerland
> And Malkyn with a distaff in her hand.
> Ran cow and calf and even the very hogs
> so feared for the barking of the dogs.
> And shouting men and women too ....
> The ducks cried as though men would them kill,
> The geese for fear flown over the trees
> Out of the hive came the swarm of bees
> So hideous was the noise.

> * coleworts or kale

2 Garden Features

Covered Walks and Arbours

Shady and concealed corners add to the charm of any garden, and shade was particularly important to fifteenth-century ladies whose pale complexion was prized. A single tree, sometimes shading a small herber, was nature's sun umbrella. Trees around the edge of a lawn, or which stood in rows either side of an orchard path, also formed a shady avenue. Loggias too, attached to buildings, and also summerhouses and cloisters, gave protection from the sun.

Flat-topped pergolas which were constructed from timber or from tree trunks also formed a canopy over paths, as did one of the most commonly illustrated features, the tunnel arbour. Such an arbour which was semi-circular in section and which sometimes incorporated a higher domed seating area, was created from coppiced poles of willow or hazel. The poles would have been renewed every two to six years. A more durable softwood juniper is also mentioned in sixteenth-century documents although yew saplings would have been more easily available. Such tunnels were virtually giant baskets, and illustrations show the joints tied with 'withies' (p. 50).

A pergola is adequate for vines, where single vine trunks can be tied to the supports before branching out over the roof. Where roses are to be incorporated, however, or where vines branch from the base in order to enclose the sides completely, the basket type of arbour is necessary for tying in shoots, with the poles set at about eighteen inch intervals. Such a tunnel arbour has been created in Queen Eleanor's Garden and at the Shrewsbury Quest. Sometimes, where a combination of vines and roses was grown, an open-sided pergola gave support to the vines, with additional side trellises about four feet high being used as a framework for the roses. This gave a vaulted effect, first described in writing by the sixteenth-century author of *The Gardeners Labyrinth*: 'having windows properly made toward the garden whereby they might more fully view and delight in the whole beauty of the garden'.

A tunnel arbour of poles or laths supporting vines and shading a path. (Illustration of a Boccaccio tale in which a lady is accused of killing her lover with poisoned sage. To prove her innocence she eats the plant but dies. A venomous toad is later found beneath the sage bush.) Flemish, *c.*1440.

Vines and roses were the most usual plants for medieval arbours, and ivy, honeysuckle and gourds were also possibilities, giving a softer and less manipulated mood to the garden than the tightly clipped hawthorn of later Tudor arbours. The climbing *Rosa alba* can be fanned out over the sides and top to a height of about eight feet; the shorter *Rosa gallica* can be induced to grow to six feet in an aged plant, but is better kept to three to four feet, when it can even be clipped as a hedge.

Seats

Seats were essential to the small medieval garden or herber and were variously named as banks, 'banckes' or benches, with medieval illustrations commonly showing them used by pairs of lovers or a Madonna and Child. The words arise from a confluence of meanings, either as a man-made bank or as a seat without a back, originating from the French *banque*. Sometimes garden illustrations show a meal being eaten, and this would be a 'banquet' in the earliest sense of the word, that is a light repast of wine and fruit between meals or as a conclusion to meals, and often eaten on the garden benches. The subject is a lesson in how much a feature is liable to be underestimated if its presence is judged on the basis of building documents alone. On the one hand references to their actual construction are rare, yet on the other they are continually quoted in literature and from 1400 onwards are illustrated in art more frequently than any other garden element.

Seats or benches in the form of raised turf-covered banks are first mentioned in 1260 by Albertus Magnus, and he advocates positioning them beside a grassy area. There are no contemporary instructions for building them, although turves brought in for their construction are occasionally mentioned. However the simplest method is to cut a vertical face and a horizontal surface into a natural bank. Banks of this type are illustrated in several Dürer etchings of seated countrywomen, and they also appear in reality in the levelled sites of the re-created Bayleaf and Hangleton gardens at the Weald and Downland Museum. William Shakespeare immortalised such a bank in *A Midsummer Night's Dream* Act II, Scene 2:

> I know a bank whereon the wild thyme blows,
> Where oxslips and the nodding violet grows
> Quite over-canopied with luscious woodbine,
> With sweet musk-roses, and with eglantine….

This description could equally well have referred to man-made built-up turf banks specifically made as seats, which were then covered with a layer of turf which might also contain other natural turf plants such as daisies, selfheal, speedwell, ground ivy, and ladies' bedstraw. However, the first real evidence of camomile being used as a seat top is post-medieval. The seats built at Odiham Castle in *c.*1332 can be interpreted in this way (Colvin, II, 1963, p. 768). Such banks can be more of a sloping-sided mound as in an illustration of the anonymous poem *The Pearl*, but are often portrayed as straight-sided blocks, which can be created by stacking turves layer upon layer, and finally pegging turf on to the upright faces. These benches are difficult to maintain in an attractive, freshly green condition, and were possibly specially carpeted with new turf for the visit of an owner – the equivalent of a

A castle garden showing an exedra-style seat and simple 'fount', or well. The trestle table would have been positioned after the group was seated. German, 15th century.

flower show effect – but they would be adequate in a brown state for spectators of archery or bowls. Benches or banks are also illustrated with the base built in the form of a timber, brick or stone box, which was then filled with rubble and soil and topped with either turf or ornamental scented plants. The seats could also be composed entirely of stone, a strikingly twentieth-century effect being displayed in Memlinc's painting *The Virgin and Child with Angel, c.*1473 (National Gallery, 686). Ladies in illustrations often give the impression of sitting directly on turf or even on plants, if a cushion is not visible. However, referring to the many copies of the original Albertus text (p. 16), we can conclude that sitting places were to be prepared on these beds, perhaps as stone slabs or timber set in to the top between the plants, as well as giving support to the front. Additional protection would also be given by the fur which lined the outer garment of sophisticated ladies, not far removed from its original function as a damp-proofing layer for animals!

Even when benches are not free-standing there is rarely a back support, the trellises of prickly roses acting as a screen rather than a seat-back, but in some illustrations close-board fencing could act as a backrest, an idea also suggested for the garden at Rhuddlan Castle (p. 128). If a back support was required a person could sit on the ground, resting on floor cushions with laced-on covers, and leaning against the seat. The benches are often in the form of a U-shape, or exedra, and one way of explaining these structures perhaps lies in an anonymous sixteenth-century description of a group of ladies who met in an arbour to discuss wedding plans. The servants then came and set up trestle tables before the seated women. The benched area could become a cosy corner for an amorous couple, using the exedra as the winged head of a bed. Some exedras have the form of a partially open hexagon or octagon, where people could gather around a multi-sided table with additional portable stools drawn up (Harvey, 1981, fig.76). A delightful further development is shown in the fifteenth-century illustration of the *Roman de la Rose* (p. 8). Here the hexagonal exedra encloses an area large enough to accommodate the six couples required for the *Carole* singing circle dance. The ladies could then return to the six lower seats cut into the bank, with the gentlemen sitting at the higher level, or resting at their feet. Single chairs were made only for royalty (Harvey, 1981, figs 21, 22). Occasionally benches assumed the proportions of a single or even a double bed, or even a short bed on which to lie curled up.

Every medieval garden has a place to sit in the shade. Seats were sometimes placed near a tree or even built in a circle round its trunk, and kept in place by a wattle front, or poles as in the Shrewsbury Quest garden. They were also situated under pole arbours of vines and roses, or even under a half-tester canopy. Stone or wooden seats were found in loggias or free-standing wooden summer houses

(Harvey, 1981, figs 56, 57). Pots of scented lilies, pinks, carnations or juniper were often placed on the seat and one wonders whether the then-known contraceptive quality of juniper was merely implied in art or whether the plant itself was sometimes actually available to a couple.

Plant Beds and Paths

Almost everyone associates medieval gardens with 'raised beds'. However William Lawson, who wrote with sixteenth-century experience, would not have been the first to note that beds could be built up or sunk according to drying out of soil, drainage conditions or availability of water. There were indeed raised beds of seat height, not only topped with turf, but even filled with flowering plants. The majority of beds, however, were built only a few inches higher than the intervening paths, with the sides supported by an edging of wattle, timber, stone or tiles enclosing rectangular areas. Aesthetically, this has a better appearance than being flush with the paths, but the more important reason is that the path itself has to be contained as much as the bed. Where beds and turf were adjacent, the beds were not raised. In kitchen gardens or for field crops where beds were annually redefined, the paths were merely trampled soil, which became depressed a little below the level of the plots between.

A further reason for raising the soil above the paths became apparent in re-creating the gardens at Bayleaf and at Hangleton (at the Weald and Downland Museum). In the place where herb beds had been planned the soil had been excavated to the flint and chalk subsoil in the course of levelling for a nearby building, and extra soil had to be added to the beds to give sufficient rooting depth. This must have been an almost universal problem in the vicinity of medieval buildings, which were continually being rebuilt on the same site in slightly varying positions. On such sites soil would have become so scarce that it would be scraped off the path areas into contained beds, augmented by scourings from ditches. The well-defined beds only a few feet in width, which are displayed in medieval Paignton (see illustration p. 45) can probably be explained in this way.

Bed widths were based on the extent of a man's reach, four to five feet being an optimum width (see p. 91). In my own kitchen garden the four five-feet wide beds which I had trampled out soon became narrower, although a taller gardener could reach across wider beds. The principle is more important than exactness of measurement, but in the re-creation of gardens the designer has to choose an average width. Length could vary, beds sometimes being square, set in gravel paths and raised a few inches, or unraised in turf, sometimes even forming an alternating chequer-board pattern of beds and turf for no apparent practical reason. Sometimes beds of quite random sizes are illustrated, set in turf paths. Both of these arrangements have been convincingly interpreted at Tretower Court (p. 119).

Beds would not have been found in the orchard where beauty lay mainly in trees, grass and shady walks, nor in the 'little park' designed for observing animals and birds. They were instead limited to the utilitarian garden, and to the herber. In the herber the free-standing beds, filled with a mixture of plants, performed the function of a herbaceous border, as judged from fourteenth- and fifteenth-century illustrations. The first indication of a rudimentary perimeter border comes in one only two feet six inches wide in the St Gall physic garden, followed by the thirteenth-century description of Albertus Magnus, where he states that around the lawn there should be grown plants which are scented and of visual beauty, which we would now call herbaceous. A perimeter border is also implied in the fourteenth-century Square Garden of Henry the Poet (Harvey, 1987). The full-blown twentieth-century border which cannot be reached across, resplendent with a huge variety of flowers in bloom from April to October would have amazed 'a northern-European medieval observer. Such borders are a result of plant introductions and breeding and are made possible by an anchored lifestyle. However it is worth mentioning in passing the totally different tradition of the medieval

LEFT *A double herber of a castle or fortified manor house.* Raised beds and herbaceous borders are in the background. In the foreground the turf and the turf-topped box stone seat both contain a variety of realistic wild flowers. The U-shape of the seat could contain a trestle table. A plank gate separates the two areas. River and park scene in the background. Flemish, late 15th century.

RIGHT *A tapestry* millefleurs *mead*, with 26 identifiable garden and woodland plants of all seasons. It is the last in a series of seven magnificent tapestries and was embroidered as a wedding gift. The unicorn represents both the captured bridegroom and Christ 'captured' by the Virgin Mary. Late 15th century.

Hispano-Arab type of garden, an example of which is to be seen at the Generalife in Granada in Spain. Here, in the sun-baked Patio de la Acequia, the borders of 10 x 75 feet which are now reconstructed at the level of the water channel between them, were in the thirteenth century sunk eighteen inches below the channel, and irrigation water seeped through holes in the tiled channel sides. A twelfth-century poem, mentioning such features, describes a mixed border of herbaceous and shrubby plants, with a few trees such as *Citrus*, well in advance of anything similar in northern Europe in the Middle Ages (Dickie, 1968).

Paths between the beds, between areas of grass, and under tunnel arbours, were of turf, gravel or sand, the two latter probably grading into each other. The materials used would have been those which were most accessible locally, and no doubt, as is known for classical gardens, gravel could gradually become softly turfed with 'weeds'. Stone and ornamentally tiled paths are occasionally illustrated.

Turf and Flowery Meads

Most people think of 'flowery meads' in connection with medieval gardens, but the prizing of pure green turf is less expected. We know that both in the code of chivalry and in the eyes of religious writers the colour green had a spiritual importance (p. 36). It is not surprising to find, therefore, that Albertus Magnus, in 1260, extolled a well-kept lawn, and gave instructions for its laying as follows (trans. Harvey, 1981):

The sight is in no way so pleasantly refreshed as by fine and close grass kept short. It is impossible to produce this except with rich and firm soil; so it behoves a man who would prepare the site for a pleasure garden, first to clear it well from the roots of weeds, which can scarcely be done unless the roots are first dug out and the site levelled, and the whole well flooded with boiling water so that the fragments of roots and seeds remaining in the earth may not by any means sprout forth. Then the whole plot is to be covered with rich turf of flourishing grass, beaten down with broad wooden mallets and trodden into the ground until they can scarcely be perceived. For then little by little they may spring forth closely and cover the surface like a green cloth.

A green lawn was still admired in the fifteenth century by an anonymous secular poet in *The Floure and the Leafe* (Pearsall, ed., 1962):

freshly turved, whereof the green grass
so small, so thick, so short, so fresh of hew
that most like unto green velvet it was.

Turves could be bought by the thousand, and in dry weather were sometimes carefully watered. In a herber for Eleanor of Castile at Conway we read that in July

1272 one of her squires was paid 3d to water at night time two cartloads of turves which had been newly laid in June (Colvin, 1963).

Whilst pure grass might have been the initial aim we know that the daisy was one of the most commonly quoted flowers, and there are records of moss being extracted from cloister turf, so garden turf might ultimately have become similar to daisied fine wild-flower turf which is now being valued round our most commonly surviving medieval building, the parish church. Such turf today is rich in the tiniest wild flowers, such as speedwells, birdsfoot-trefoil, thyme, hawkbits, ladies' bed-straw, and self-heal, growing according to the soil and closeness of mowing. It should be understood that the expert medieval gardener could have scythed as closely as his nineteenth-century counterpart in a Scottish bowling club, who in turn considered his scything to be superior to the first mechanical lawn mowers.

As distinct from such lawns and flowering turf, the term 'flowery mead' is a present-day expression for a carpet bejewelled with flowers as depicted in medieval paintings and in the *millefleurs* backgrounds of tapestries, mainly of the fifteenth century. Such a mead is also frequently alluded to in poetry. In art the flowers were set against a green background, the most commonly selected being those which were easy to portray, such as the daisy or composite type, cowslip, straw-berry, and violas. Secondly, those which produced a neat leaf rosette, such as plan-tains or the dandelion type were shown, as were those of particular symbolism, such as the threefold leaf of the strawberry, the heart-shaped leaf of the violet or the entwining periwinkle. Once chosen by the artist, particular attention was paid to aesthetically regular spacing, in contrast to natural meadows, where different species grow in ever-shifting clumps. The artist's mead is also timeless, depicting each plant in its flowering prime, primrose of spring, rose of high summer, and car-nation of late summer nestling side by side, destined to create a winter garden on a draughty castle wall. The richest portrayals include more than carpeting plants since, in addition to the low ground cover of periwinkle and strawberry, a Madonna can often be seen sitting amongst taller plants of a herbaceous type such as peony, iris, lily-of-the-valley, and columbine. In tapestries as many as a hundred species can be identified, even in the incomplete *Tausendblumenteppich* tapestry in the Historisches Museum in Berne (which is being planted there). The richest portray-al of the different plants, which gave rise to the true *millefleurs* flowery mead, can be seen in the seven exquisite Unicorn tapestries at the Cloisters Museum in New York (one is illustrated on p. 55). Here in different habitats of almost photographic accuracy over one hundred plants, of which eighty-five have been identified, are woven into every space between the huntsmen. There are dark ancient woodlands with butcher's broom, betony, orchids and ferns; riverside plants such as iris and bulrush reflected in the water; and garden plants beside the fountain, such as the red rose and wallflower. All these come together in a grand crescendo in the true *millefleurs* background of the seventh tapestry on which the Unicorn rests.

This latter glimpse of the medieval countryside, as seen through the artist's eye, gives us a clue as to where to look for flowering meads in their medieval reality, through which lovers, churchmen and peasants alike could stroll. Even as now, there were hazel coppices in parks, which could nurture as many as 300 species, and arable field edges where swathes of colourful cornfield annuals, such as mauve corn cockle, blue cornflower, yellow corn marigold and red corn poppy, grew in dense profusion. There were hay fields, at their richest in June, with perennials such as ox-eye daisies, yellow rattle, knapweeds and scabious, before being mown for hay. Such turf was found also in orchards, where an additional cut refined the grass, allowing spring flowers such as cowslips to grow. There were kitchen gardens where pot marigold, wild camomile, mauve garden poppies and blue borage self-seeded thickly to produce a glowing carpet. In herbers the ubiquitous wild strawberry and the lowly periwinkle formed a dense mat beneath the roses, and these, together with speedwell and ladies' bedstraw, could form a carpet in a small herber, or even a dense ground cover between shrubby peonies in the borders. Thus if we unweave the complex *millefleurs* tapestry and restore the plants to their different habitats we find that there were in reality many types of flowering mead in the medieval countryside and garden.

Fountains and Ornamental Pools

The meanings of the words fount, springhead or wellspring are clear enough to us, implying a source of water and, by symbolic extension, a source of life, wisdom or cleansing. However, it is not always obvious what was meant in documents. The word *fons* could mean a springhead, but also a fountain. Even when an author has used the word 'fontaine', as in the French *Roman de la Rose*, both Chaucer as translator and also some illustrators interpret this as 'welle'. The word 'well' also implies a 'welling up' and therefore a spring. The freestone font which is proudly documented by the wealthy but not aristocratic thirteenth-century Henry de Bray may have been nothing more than an ornamented wellhead.

Whatever the form of a spout or fountain there has to be a natural or artificial water supply leading to it from a higher level, and if the supply is greater than the volume of the pool an overflow to a lower level is also required, even if it is not visible. Both in the Eastern and in the medieval Christian tradition this idea of a trinity is reflected in the design of fountains. The three states of water, namely the bubbling, sparkling source or spout, the shallow moving sheet, and the still, silent

April in a herber. A four-jet fountain is topped by a bronze image. Water flows through two lion-head masks into a pool or stream. A child picks daisies from the turf. Beyond the latticed railings a falconer walks past a pentice. Behind there is a spy tower typical of a falcon mews. Flemish, early 16th century.

pool are expressed in three ancient Persian concepts related to garden water features: the arrival, the mysterious veil and the static mirror (Tabbana,1987). A Christian trinity is also recognised by Guillaume de Machaut in his *Laye de la Fonteinne c.*1350 in praise of the Virgin, whom he equates with the fountain (trans. William Earle Nettles):

Three parts make up a fountain flow
The Stream, the Spout, the bowl.
Although these are three, these three are one
Essence the same.
Even so the Waters of Salvation run.

Few medieval garden fountains still exist, and references are rare in construction documents, although from the fifteenth century onwards examples are frequent in poetry, painting and manuscript illustration. In Christian art there is a not unexpected emphasis on a gothic style, and in secular art there is more emphasis on fluted bowls, spheres and baths, with plant, animal, shell, crown and spiral motifs, some having an Islamic, and some a Byzantine origin. In southern Europe fine examples of the latter styles can be seen in the Court of Lions in the Alhambra, Granada, and in the monastery cloister in Monreale, respectively.

There are no extant northern European fountains so the documentation for an ornamental fountain at Charing Cross Mews Westminster, dating from 1275, is of great value. Here the water was brought by aqueduct from neighbouring land and it poured through four leopard-head spouts into a lead pool, the whole structure surmounted by a bronze falcon. The re-created fountain in Queen Eleanor's Garden, Winchester, is based on this example, where it has been interpreted in a gothic style, involving the three states of water already mentioned. However lion-type masks are found in gothic, Islamic and Byzantine styles, and since falconry had Arab origins

'Pineapple' or pinecone fountain column, showing a Byzantine influence. In the background are a variety of specimen trees and clipped shrubs. The radiating paths and a possible menagerie, implied by the escaped lion, suggest a park scene, probably from Hesdin. (Here Pyramis commits suicide on seeing Thisbe's blood-stained clothing.) Flemish, 1461.

one could equally argue a case for a Moorish style at the Mews, perhaps even as remembered by Eleanor of Castile, herself, in her native land. Water is essential for falcons who need to dampen their feathers before flight and a flat tin or wooden bowl is sufficient, but in this London Mews in medieval times a simple need was elevated to high art.

Judging from building documents, small pools were probably more common than fountains, in Britain. A prime example is the 'three pools in chain' at Rosamund's Bower at Blenheim Palace which were most likely to have been set at successively lower levels, connected by a flow of water. One of these pools has, incidentally, survived, at the margin of Capability Brown's enlarged lake. Such pools contained fish, as did many others, for which payment is recorded, but paintings often show structures such as small bathing pools. Illustrations usually reveal fine ashlar kerbs cramped with metal stays. Lead or clay were the most common lining materials, and water inlets and outlets and associated channels are often seen, which would help to keep the water flowing and pure.

Garden Sundries from the Countryside

Many garden materials came from the managed 'coppice and standard' type of wood described on p. 106. Apart from fuel, and a wide variety of house-building timber and materials, these woods provided the most common garden necessities. The stoutest carpenter-worked building timber was produced from the tall unknotted trunks of the oak. Younger oak and poles of ash were felled and adzed to produce square posts 3–6 inches in diameter for internal walls, minor garden buildings and ornamental fence posts of wealthy households. Oak plank wood, 1–2 inches thick, for close-board fencing and garden bed edges of the wealthy was sawn by means of saw-pits and two-handled saws, one man above ground and an apprentice below, with sawdust in his eyes. It could also be cleaved.

Shingles necessary for tiling minor roofs including garden pentices (as at Queen Eleanor's Garden) were split from small trunk blocks 8–10 inches long; oak laths about $\frac{1}{8}$ inch thick, and 1–2 inches wide were produced by longitudinal splitting of the lower truck. The maximum length of laths today is about four feet six inches, which can be incorporated into diagonal lath fencing up to about four feet high (for example, the Shrewsbury Quest railings or the Bayleaf vegetable garden gate). Higher fencing has therefore to be built in two tiers, as is sometimes illustrated in medieval documents. Poles were necessary not only for the wattle and daub walls of buildings: exactly the same wattle was used undaubed, not only for garden sheds, sheep folds and animal pens, but the very fences themselves. Such poles – our present-day bean pole – were produced from coppiced ash and hazel, cut during winter before the sap rose and made them brittle. In damp places osier rods were also available, and these were required for semi-circular tunnel arbours too. One-year-old osier rods were cut in winter and twisted to break the fibres, making 'withies' which acted as string or wire for tying railings, vines and roses. A finer 'bass', as still available today, was produced from the inner bark of lime trees. The best brushwood was used for besom brooms and the pickings were incorporated in newly laid hedges to protect the young shoots, any forked branch being carefully hoarded for a variety of uses.

Certain stages in the coppice cycle produced abundant hawthorn, ash, maple and holly seedlings which were necessary for establishing new hedges. Finally the coppice edges supplied many of the plants grown in gardens, and there are records as late as those of Henry VIII which mention violets, primroses and wild strawberry being planted from the woods. Annual scourings from the ditches made rich garden soil.

A wealthy owner would obtain these supplies from his own hunting parks, or perhaps a spinney within his garden, as at Cuxham. A yeoman living in wooded country would have his small fields surrounded by such copses or 'shaws', and perhaps his homestead, as is being developed at Bayleaf. A lord would give even a peasant tenant the right to 'fencebote' (fencing materials).

One way and another, basic sundries were available for all classes of society from coppiced woods.

Boundaries and Fences

From the time of King Alfred it was imperative that all properties should have a cattle-proof boundary. Ditches of varying width and depth outlined many properties ranging from moats as much as thirty yards wide to ditches four feet wide. Stone walls were rare and prestigious, and cob walls made of clay and straw are occasionally recorded (Harvey, P.D.A., 1965). Fences and hedges, however, were the most common horticultural boundaries, the two words often being indistinguishable in meaning, and a deadwood structure could become a living hedge as a result of interplanting or natural seeding.

The earliest description of this hedging process is known from the Roman invasion of Flanders, where 'the native tribes half-cut young trees and bent them. With the brambles and young thorns growing up, these hedges present a barrier like a wall either to penetrate or see through' (Caesar's *Gallic Wars*, Book II, ch. 17). Even today this primitive type of hedging is used to protect new growth after coppicing of woodland. A more refined form of this method was the basis of the majority of the hedges which still exist today, about half of which are survivors from the Middle Ages. The essence of the process is ditching, and banking, quicksetting and protecting with brushwood, followed by later 'laying', as explained in the following paragraph.

We have to wait until the sixteenth century for exact details of how hedges were constructed. Fitzherbert, writing in 1534, with forty years' experience, states that the ditch could be as small as four feet across and two feet six inches deep, sufficient to prevent cattle approaching the hedge. Stakes could be positioned on its bank up to two feet six inches apart, made from heart of oak, crabtree, blackthorn or alder. Ash and maple were less durable but saplings of these and also oak could be planted for future coppicing, at ten to twelve feet apart, in the fence. The tops of the stakes were 'eddered' or woven together with long rails of hazel or willow, and the fence was planted during the winter with seedlings of hawthorn, crabtree, and holly, and protected against sheep by brushwood. After about ten years, when the dead fence turned to living hedge, the base became bare, so the hedge was 'laid', that is, the stems of the original shrubs were half-cut at the base, and bent to an angle of forty-five degrees, some being left uncut and trimmed as posts, at two- to three-feet intervals. The tops were woven together with each other and with new eddering rails, the whole process being known as pleaching or plashing. New shoots sprung up along the newly sloping branch and from the half-cut base, and were again

A typical managed wood in December. The photographic quality of this early 16th-century Flemish miniature shows the exact nature of a coppice with standards, or virgultum. *Trees for building have been felled in the foreground, others remain as ash and oak standards. Behind can be seen dense 7-to-10-year-old hazel stools.*

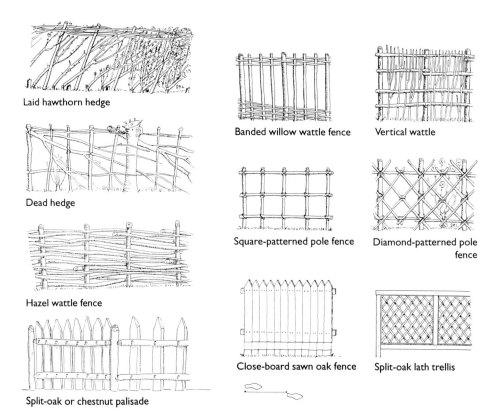

Types of hedging and fencing

Laid hawthorn hedge

Dead hedge

Hazel wattle fence

Split-oak or chestnut palisade

Banded willow wattle fence

Vertical wattle

Square-patterned pole fence

Diamond-patterned pole fence

Close-board sawn oak fence

Split-oak lath trellis

protected by brushwood. Such hedges might last another twenty years before the process was repeated.

Specific examples of such ditching, cutting, pleaching and protecting appear in fourteenth-century accounts, with hawthorn seedlings bought by the thousand (Harvey, 1981). This labour-intensive process was repeated through the centuries, and it is still demonstrated in its various stages at the Weald and Downland Museum. In medieval times ditching and hedging protected not only farm enclosures, but also newly sown oak woods and gardens (Harvey, 1981). Even in urban locations the gardens of the Hull plan show hedges (see p. 33) and they can be seen in the tiny gardens in plans of Wilton and Paignton (see p. 45). The process is documented for a twelve-acre enclosure in Wiltshire which was carved out of woodland in 1251–3 (Titow,1969):

In digging 3751 yards of ditch 7 feet wide, 6 foot deep. £7.2s.1d
In plants for the bank. 18s.11d

| In stakes at 18 inch intervals. | 14s. |
| In making the enclosure, gathering and carrying brushwood for it. | 51s. 9½d |

The bank of a nearby enclosure ditch was planted with willows at three-feet intervals, to supply replacement coppice stakes and rods as well as protection.

For many peasant village closes, however, replacement 'fencebote' for dead hedges (which the peasants were obliged to maintain) was usually built into the tenancy contract and many an elderly woman could haul in and build a crude dead pole and brushwood fence, as noted by Chaucer in the *Nun's Priest's Tale*:

> A yerd she hadde, enclosed al aboute
> With stikkes, and a drye dych with-oute.

If adequate coppice poles were grown on an estate then a woven wattle fence could be constructed from hazel, which would last between six and eight years. The stockyard fencing and palings for the deer parks of the wealthy were made from upright half-round logs or split-oak planks, and fixed with cross bars, which were attached by square oak pegs driven into awled round holes. When such fencing was placed on top of a scarp, as now seen at Bayleaf, or on a high bank, as in the medieval deer parks, economies were made in the height of the timber, with the height and sturdiness of fencing depending on the need for it. A total bank and fence height of nine feet was necessary to keep deer in or out, four feet six inches for cattle, three feet for sheep, and three feet of flints or a water-filled ditch to keep rabbits contained in special warrens. It may be that the probable ditched orchard site of Conegar (Coneygarth), which can still be seen at St Cross Hospital, Winchester, is a surviving example of a medieval hedged and ditched enclosure (Currie, 1992). Evidence for a variety of fencing and boundaries is known from an archaeological investigation at Hangleton, Sussex (Holden, 1963; Hurst, 1964), and rubble banks and ditches have been found on deserted sites, for example at Wharram Percy in Yorkshire (Beresford and Hurst, 1990).

Subdivisions within gardens were built with the same materials used on a more refined scale, since privacy or attractive support for vines and roses was more important than fencing against animals. Hedges in small herbers, for instance, were of hawthorn, interwoven with native hedge plants such as honeysuckle and sweet briar. They were maintained with great artistry (Pearsall, ed., 1962):

> Wrethen in fere so well and cunningly
> That every branch and leaf grew by mesure
> Plain as a bord ….

The Floure and the Leafe, anon.

Low fences of between three and four feet were used to edge paths and make small enclosures. The main materials were hazel, willow, birch and alder. A wattle of basket-like finish could be achieved with willow canes, grown as coppiced osiers, in either a solid or banded pattern. A more crude vertical wattling was sometimes seen. Poles of varying thickness were also tied with withies in square or diagonal patterns, and both these and wattled fences could be used as trellises for roses. Cleft-oak lath of one to two inches in width was also used for fencing, and by the late fifteenth century the pillars were sometimes finished by turned knobs. Recreated effects can be seen in the cloister at Christ Church, Oxford, and at Tretower Court, Powys, and split-oak lath is used at the Shrewsbury Quest.

Rivers, Moats and Fishponds

Not only 'Capability' Brown's park-like clumps of trees, but even more, his lakes, had a forerunner in medieval times. The names for water features, such as *stew, stank, stagnum,* or even *fishpond*, have caused us to underestimate their aesthetic value, as distinct from function, and we are only now beginning to see medieval man as a manipulator of water for beauty and status, as well as for breeding of fish and wildfowl, perhaps unequalled in later garden styles. Moats and pools surrounded the properties of the nobility, and lower down the social scale, even peasants' dwellings were sometimes bordered by water-filled ditches.

LEFT *Joseph and the Angel.* The artist chose a trellised herber to show Joseph as carpenter, with brace and bit, and awl for making dowel holes. Mary sits on a trellised turf seat beyond. The border uniquely depicts daffodils. Flemish, *c.*1450.

These features were intricately bound up with springs and rivers, since flowing water was necessary in order to avoid stagnation. A faith in the beneficent nature of flowing water is revealed in a thirteenth-century account which describes the harnessing of river water at the monastery of Clairvaux. A channel was diverted from the River Aube 'made not by nature, but by the labour of monks', and then with 'the sluice acting as a porter, [the water] makes its first assault upon the mill, then apportioning itself among a number of arms it diligently enquires everywhere what task has need of it – cooking, sieving, turning, grinding, washing, softening'. On its way one channel watered a garden which was divided into small areas by streams flowing between them. Here 'the water serves a dual purpose of nurturing fish and irrigating vegetables …. Finally bearing away the refuse it leaves everything spick and span and it hurries back to the river, all together once more' (Braunfels, 1972).

MOATS   Many castles were surrounded by ditches and high defensive banks, but moats without banks were a feature of domestic residences. Remains of moats mainly constructed between 1150–1325, are to be found over most of north-west Europe. The labour involved in moating was enormous and an enclosed acre would require the manual removal of some 2500 cubic metres of earth (Aberg, 1978).

Moats have been roughly defined as not less than five yards wide and a minimum of six feet deep. The majority of those which have survived are rectangular, square or trapezoidal, with some being conjoined, as at Alvechurch in Worcestershire, others being concentric, as at Kenilworth, or Hawton in Northamptonshire, and at Peterborough Abbey. They were often formed by damming as at Bodiam, rather than labour intensive excavating, and they did not always form a complete ring, leaving a causeway crossing rather than a bridge, as at Somersham Palace in Cambridgeshire.

Moats were situated on the flood plain beside a river, or were sometimes perched at a higher level on the valley side. Some, as at Bodiam Castle in Sussex, were fed by springs, but many were connected to a river by an inlet leat or channel,

RIGHT *Boating.* The flat-bottomed boats were punted or paddled. At dawn on May Day hawthorn or birch branches were gathered. Flemish, 1526.

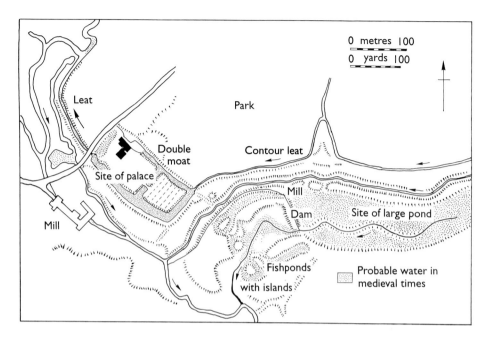

the water returning to the river through an outlet leat, as described for Clairvaux. A most striking piece of detective work (shown left) has revealed that the conjoined double moat at Alvechurch was ingeniously supplied by, and re-connected to, the River Arrow by a long channel following the valleyside contours but flowing in the opposite direction to the river in some stretches (Aston, 1970).

Large moats, often without a residence on them, enclosed islands which contained herbers, an orchard, pavilions, or perhaps the possibility of a utilitarian garden or even a menagerie. One of the most beautiful herbers, for

Bishop's Palace, Alvechurch, Worcestershire. The double-moated palace is perched high on the valley side, and fed by an inlet and outlet channel. A large mill pond once existed, with fishponds at its dam, each with an island. Orchards or kitchen gardens could have been laid out within the moated areas.

which there is both written and illustrated evidence was the one at Peterborough Abbey, of some two acres, double-moated and surrounded by pear trees and '*herbis delicatissimis*' (Harvey, 1981).

It is not clear to what extent domestic moats were built as a defence against intruders, but they were certainly a safeguard against the ravages of ubiquitous deer and were also a means of keeping valuable livestock from straying or being stolen. We now take tapped water and drains for granted, but moats were probably associated with a raised standard of living in days before water was otherwise available only from rivers and streams. Here was a source literally on the doorstep, for clothes-washing, bathing and sewage disposal. Moats provided ideal conditions for growing ever-useful willows, rushes and watermints along their banks, as well as for breeding fish, fowl and swans, and in addition they saved increasingly scarce fencing materials.

FISHPONDS   Fish was an important part of the medieval diet, as water and air-borne creatures were favoured for their purity, above terrestrial livestock. The Bible stated: 'And God said unto Adam, "Cursed is the ground for thy sake"' (Gen. III, 17), and fish were thus deemed to have escaped Adam's curse. The purpose of fasting was abstinence from anything sinful, hence only fish, with their property of purity, were eaten on the numerous fasting days which amounted to over half the year. Fridays, usually Wednesdays and Saturdays, all holy days, the eve of major church feasts, six weeks in Lent and four weeks before Advent were all days of fasting. A royal account for the resident family of eight together with the servants at King's Langley neatly demonstrates the difference between a fast and a feast day (*Archaeologia* XV):

KING'S LANGLEY – 1290

Fast Day Passion Sunday, Lent		Feast Day Easter Sunday	
200 Haberdens Salt [cod]	4 gross, eels	¼ beef	6 chickens
300 Herrings	1 pickerel	1 mutton	12 pigeons
3 gallons, oysters	5 sticks, eels [smoked]	1 bacon	450 eggs
3 congers	trout	½ hog	
whelks	salmon	1½ calves	
8 salmon pasties	mustard	2 kids	
barley for the camel		barley and hay for the camel	

Sea fish and eels, particularly in their long-lasting salted or dried form, appeared on the platter with monotonous regularity, so, as a contrast, river fish such as bream, pike, perch and roach were carefully bred to enhance the diet of the wealthy.

Two types of pond were required for fish management, the large *vivarium* or breeding pond (which was often a lake) and a small *servatorium* or storage pond. This was the reverse of later fish management. The fish were introduced into the *vivarium*, often as a gift, in a breeding state, having been carefully transported in wet rushes. Both ponds required slowly flowing water, controlled by a side channel, which helped to prevent silting up and they were drained about every five years by means of a timber sluice which was 'broken open', the fish then being sorted and any clay lining and hurdle side supports repaired. Fish were netted by boat from the large pools and transferred to the small storage ponds where they could even be caught from the sides, such pools commonly becoming an ornamental garden feature in the pleasure garden (Currie, 1990). They were usually walled or hedged to prevent theft, a wall close to a pond also preventing herons from landing and stealing the fish.

Large monastic fishponds, sometimes doubling as millponds, were thought to have been necessary to supply the fish-dominated diet of monks, but it has been

A storage-type fishpond. The sluice could be 'broken' to drain the pond, every few years. The railing would be close-hurdled under the water to prevent the fish being drained out, so that they could be periodically sorted. Flemish, 15th century.

calculated that at least two acres of water would be necessary to breed a daily half pound of fish for each monk. Rather, the monastic pool was a symbol of prestige, its fish being used only on special feast days (Currie, 1988). These pools were often referred to as the Abbot's pool and were sometimes made at great inconvenience to the monastery. Jocelyn de Brakelond, the twelfth-century chronicler, with a sharp eye for human foibles, tells a revealing story of the abbot of Bury St Edmunds in 1182, determined to have his own pool so that he too, like royalty, could dispense favours. 'He raised the fishpond of Babwell by the new mill to such a height that there is no man rich or poor beside the waterside from Towngate to Eastgate but

Wild fowl around a nobleman's lake. This illustration emphasises the value of pools such as that at Kenilworth Castle for wild fowl and sport as well as fish. Fishing, netting, shooting and using hawks and falcons to catch prey are shown. Birds are not accurately portrayed but peacock, pheasant, hawks, heron, magpie, crane, blackbird and ducks can be detected. Flemish, 15th century.

has lost his garden and orchards. The cellarer's pasture on the other side of the bank is destroyed, the cellarer's meadow ruined, the infirmarian's orchard drowned. Once the cellarer spoke in chapter, complaining, but the abbot said angrily that he was not going to lose his fishpond for the sake of our meadow.' Many monasteries also ran river fisheries commercially, and these could produce eels in their thousands.

The nobility as well as the monasteries were instructed to make the most of their pools, as advised in *Fleta*, a thirteenth-century landowner's manual: 'Every prudent man stocks his ponds, pools, lakes and reservoirs from fisheries, with bream and perch'. By the fourteenth century lower levels of society such as Chaucer's franklin also had 'many a bream and many a luce in stuwe', which had become possible with the development of the small moated manor in the thirteenth and fourteenth centuries.

One of the clearest pictures of the range of waters suitable for fish breeding and storage has been revealed by documentary and archaeological research at Kenilworth Castle (shown overleaf). The only medieval *servatorium* to survive, though alas without fish, is at the twelfth-century St Cross Hospital, Winchester. Here, as with all travellers over the last 850 years, you can still receive 'Wayfarer's dole' of token beer if you have travelled by foot

Kenilworth Castle, Warwickshire, as in medieval times, with the Great Pool for breeding fish, storage-type pools and river fisheries. The castle wall enclosed a garden area but the double-moated pleasance contained further gardens, a banqueting house and towers.

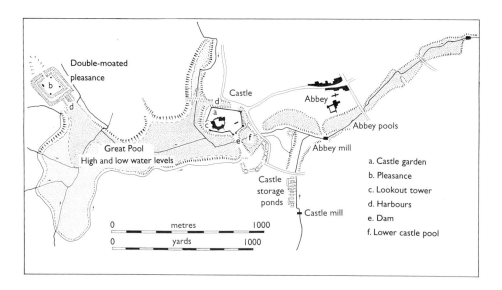

Double-moated pleasance

Castle

Abbey

Abbey pools

Abbey mill

Great Pool
High and low water levels

Castle storage ponds

Castle mill

a. Castle garden
b. Pleasance
c. Lookout tower
d. Harbours
e. Dam
f. Lower castle pool

0   metres   1000
0   yards   1000

for a token one hundred yards. The pool is about 45 by 150 feet, turf-edged, clay-lined, with a still-visible entrance silt trap and exit sluice.

The physical impact of fishponds and moats on the landscape is obvious, and their utilitarian, defensive and prestigious qualities are beyond doubt. Fishponds or lakes flanked the causeway approaches of Kenilworth, Stow Park, Somersham Palace and Woodstock Palace, and the supreme example is seen in the complex approach route to Bodiam Castle (Taylor, Everson and Wilson-North, 1990). However, the question of the extent to which their aesthetic and symbolic qualities were valued is awaiting exploration.

Dovecots

Medieval dovecots, or *columbaria*, were flint or stone towers of circular or square shape, designed to keep out rats, and they had tiled, thatched or timber lantern roofs. They were common in important households, both monastic and lay ones.

The manors of Cuxham and Harlestone each had two. The roofs of farm buildings in England no doubt also housed doves, as illustrated in numerous continental nativity paintings. The towers were constantly rebuilt since the flimsy roofs were prone to decay and the flocks themselves were killed by murrain. An artist's reconstruction of an archaeological find at Cosmeston Manor, near Cardiff, shows a revolving ladder, and a similar dovecot able to house 1000 birds, also with a central revolving ladder, can be seen at Basing House in Hampshire. In the thirteenth century there were instructions for repairing the thatched *columbaria* at Winchester

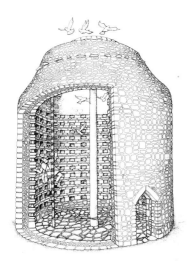

A 15th-century dovecot, or columbarium. Artist's reconstruction from archeological finds at the deserted village of Cosmeston in south Wales. Note the revolving ladder and numerous nesting boxes. There could equally have been a timber lantern at the top, with side entrances.

Castle, and today once again shy white doves fly over the site from Queen Eleanor's Garden there.

The destructive wood pigeon has always been with us, and in medieval times it counted as free warren. However the medieval dove or plain 'pigeon' is the pure white *Columba livia*, and as a garden bird it has several advantages. First, being a cave-dwelling bird originally, it takes easily to domestication if given a stone niche in a dark tower. Doves were a useful adjunct to the medieval menu since the dovecots were the counterpart of the battery-hen breeders of today. A pair of birds can rear two squabs in three to four weeks, available for the table before their first flight, and this event could be repeated several times a year. Second, the dung was top of the list as garden manure, and is mentioned in thirteenth-century estate texts. In the accounts of St Peter's, Gloucester, we read that the *columbaria* were swept out twice a year, and the dung used in the garden. The floor of the earliest identified dovecot, of the late twelfth-century, at Thornholme Priory, was scoured hollow, and had a drain leading to an outside collection tank. Thirdly the siting of the dovecot in or beside a garden is possible because the white dove, as a seed and grain eater, is not destructive to plants and the dung can thus be transferred with minimum transport.

There is, in addition, the aesthetic appeal. This view is supported by the beauty of the Thornholme Priory dovecot associated with the guesthouse, with its white plastered walls red-lined as imitation ashlar, and its hipped and tiled roof decorated with ridge tiles (Coppack, 1990). The sight of a flock of white birds wheeling in a blue sky is always breathtaking; their contented purring is one of nature's tranquilisers, and their flirting, cocking and bulling, before pairing for life, adds entertainment. It is not surprising therefore that together with the annually immigrant turtle dove they enter into garden imagery, poetry and ecclesiastical works – one white dove the symbol of the Holy Spirit, two the symbol of marriage. A full flock was a symbol of Venus, and provided a white counterpoint to the colourful human medieval court life and courtly love being acted out in the garden below.

3 The Plants

Our present-day understanding of European medieval plant names has arisen from manuscripts which were originally written in languages as diverse as Syriac, Greek, Arabic and Latin. Illustrations were only sometimes of realistic beauty, and often caricatured the plants. How therefore do we know what plants were grown in European medieval gardens? Plants, like humans, now have two Latin names, a first genus name and a second species name, and are grouped into families with common characteristics. This classification has only existed with any accuracy since the mid-eighteenth century when Linnaeus first grouped plants according to their physical features, although keeping many of the ancient names. Before this, plants had been named according to criteria such as mythological fame, Christian symbolism, a conspicuous feature, or medieval usage. A further complication arose in medicine since lists appeared of alternative plants which could be used to treat the same condition. For instance some authorities listed groups of plants which had the same uses such as 'Febrifuga', plants used to control fever, or 'Consolida', plants which 'consolidated' haemorrhages. Plants with these qualities, even if from different families, were then given the same name. Thus the name *Consolida minor* distinguished the bruisewort, or our common daisy, from *Consolida media*, our ox-eye daisy, and from *Consolida major*, which is comfrey, but comes from a different family (Harvey, 1993).

A firm basis for medieval plant names came from Greek writers, particularly Dioscorides, a botanist and pharmacologist, living at the beginning of the first century AD. The works of Dioscorides incorporated some 345 names, giving also their medical use, which were mainly released to western Europe by translation from Greek into Arabic in the Arabic translating schools of the ninth century, and from Arabic to Latin in the tenth century. Since Latin was the common European language the works became accessible to many countries, albeit in somewhat garbled form, and the plants were later given national and vernacular names as well, necessitated by the dwindling of Latin. An early sixteenth-century example of how

A bench planted with peonies and wallflowers. Behind, there is a tied-pole trellis with roses and birds. German, *c.*1450.

a plant can receive its vernacular name is given by William Turner, when collecting for his list of plants which was published in 1538. 'A little girl seven years old met me as I was walking along the road; she carried in her right hand a bunch of white flowers. I thought to myself Those are Narcissi but when I enquired the name no reply was forthcoming, so I asked the folk in the neighbouring cottages. They all answered that it was called Laus tibi, (Praise be to Thee).' No doubt through the ages this hidden mass of ordinary people, whether for aesthetic pleasure or superstitious reasons, were naming and communicating, and thus helping to build up a local vernacular plant vocabulary. The number of plants which were actually grown in northern Europe, as distinct from being imported medically in dried form, increased throughout the period and by 1500 they totalled about 300, although many of these would have been grown by herbalists and botanists only. These names from diverse sources have gradually been equated with the present-day Linnaean or later names, so that lists can now be compared throughout the ages, largely through the work of John Harvey (Harvey, 1981, onwards).

Climatic conditions had a major effect on the choice of plants for cultivation. The slight deterioration in weather from a warm eleventh-century optimum removed fruiting bottle

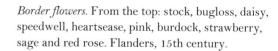

gourds from northern plant lists, and the zonal differences between the northern and southern European climate, which still exist, restricted fruiting citrus and pomegranate, palms and myrtle to the south. Comprehensive collections of plants were grown in botanic and scientific gardens by Arab botanists in eleventh-century Spain, long before this type of garden appeared further north. From these centres other Mediterranean plants filtered northwards, such as wallflower, holly-hock, lavender and *Physalis alkengi*.

The question is often posed as to whether 'all the plants' are still available. The answer is a surprising yes for almost every ornamental and medicinal species. The key flowering plants were of the present-day cottage garden type, unchanged through the centuries, such as the red and white rose, purple irises, peonies and pot marigolds. Many garden plants were of a wild form, still available today, from which a few double forms had been bred by the end of the Middle Ages, such as the granny's bonnet columbine and double common daisy. Often it is the plant rather than the flower itself which has been improved. For instance the present-day wall-flower 'Gold Bedder' or the Johnny Jump-Up form of *Viola tricolor*, as used in Queen Eleanor's garden, are unauthentic only in a neater plant form, not the flower. The medieval latecomers, the pink and the carnation are the exception. These have been developed through the ages, and are now only available as the 'jacks' of the commercial breeders – discarded throwbacks which occasionally appear, matching their medieval illustration counterpart in which key features are single or semi-double flowers with frilled petals, pink, white or red, and some-times the hint of an 'eye'.

The majority of the medicinal plants and the shrubby aromatic herbs are likely to be unchanged. Many vegetables still retain a close resemblance to original vari-eties, though no actual continuity can be traced back. Skirrets, garlic and plain-leaved parsley can still be obtained, and the medieval broad bean is well rep-resented by the horse-bean Maris Bead. The 'edible weeds' or self-seeding crops are

Border flowers. From the top: stock, bugloss, daisy, speedwell, heartsease, pink, burdock, strawberry, sage and red rose. Flanders, 15th century.

identical, being largely native. Peas, leeks and parsnips are still represented but by modern larger varieties of more perfect form and uniformity.

Bulb onions, sown or planted as sets, were available then as now in both the round and elongated form, yellow and red. However the major unresolved plant problem is the nature of the *ascalonia* and *fissiles* type of onion, and of the ambiguously termed scallion, chibol and holeke. For the time being at Bayleaf, where the outcome of the argument cannot wait, we represent scallions by any small or bull-necked bulb onions which will not keep, and are therefore pulled whilst green; the chibol and the holeke (the latter described as a clumping winter onion by William Turner) are represented by the ever-ready onion, *Allium cepa* var. *perutile.* This is not to be confused with the 'Welsh' onion (Old German *welsch* meaning 'foreign') or the true ciboule or spring onion, *Allium fistulosum,* which was a late-medieval arrival in Europe from Asia, not reaching England until the eighteenth century (Stearn, 1943). The brassicas however have changed the most. The lack of a suitable small-headed cabbage is not so important as the loss in England, only recently, of the colewort, ubiquitous in medieval times, its nearest English relative being a non-curly kale. At present in the Bayleaf re-creation we grow its nearest European equivalent, the American collard, probably introduced from Europe in the sixteenth and seventeenth centuries. This, mixed with Hungry Gap Kale, has proved to be the best way to achieve the all-year growth noted by Jon Gardener in the fourteenth century. In re-creation it is preferable to use a 'look-alike' rather than omit a basic plant.

Lists were drawn up for different reasons: administrative in the case of Charlemagne in order to ensure a relatively uniform stocking of imperial estates throughout Europe; botanical in the case of Friar Daniel, who listed 252 species growing in his garden in Stepney in the mid-fourteenth century; and medical for Henry the Poet, who was probably a physician and listed the top 96 medicinal plants for inclusion in his 'Square Garden'. Such lists look dreary but they are brought alive in exquisite manuscript paintings, and since virtually all the plants are still available a bunch of them collected from a present-day re-created medieval garden gives us a sense of the original freshness (see illustration p. 82).

The Fromond list which follows had yet another purpose, particularly useful for us. This list was compiled about 1525, probably for a royal household, but if we remove artichoke, castor oil plant, lungwort and stickadove which were late introductions, then we are left with a likely English list of around 1500, at the end of the Middle Ages. It has the unique feature of being classified according to plant use, so from our knowledge of diet and medicine we can use it as a good base from which to select species which would be grown in different levels of society. For instance

Shooting at the butts with gallery behind. This Flemish MS was presented to Henry VII in 1496. A few years later butts and galleries were built at Richmond Palace by Henry VII. Note the turf-topped bench. In the borders can be seen red rose, sweet rocket, corncockle, violet, periwinkle, lily, pinks, heartsease, double daisy and speedwell.

wealthy households would grow medicinal plants such as the pain-relieving mandrake and henbane, and plants for distilling and for herbers. On the other hand a yeoman's garden would predominantly contain the more common pottage and salad plants, and few root vegetables or plants for savour and beauty.

All lists are incomplete and a number of surprising omissions are known from Jon Gardener's royal household list of some 150 years earlier. But if these are added to the Fromond list, as well as orchard and hedging trees, the combination provides a list of plants available at the end of the fifteenth century which we can carry in our mind's eye whilst considering the architectural features and garden activities of the following pages.

THE FROMOND LIST C.1525

The original title was 'Herbys necessary for a gardyn' and the following version is taken from J. Harvey, 1989, who also gives the Latin names and discussion. Early sixteenth-century plants have been excluded.

* indicates a native plant.

( ) included in the alphabetical list of the original MS but not in the compiler's classified list.

Herbs for pottage

* Agrimony	Clary	Lettuce	Radish
* Alexanders	Colewort	Lupin	Rape
Astrologia longa	* Columbine	* Mallow	Safflower
A. rotunda	Coriander	Marigold, Pot	Sage
* Avens	* Daisy	Marjoram	Spinach
Basil	* Dandelion	* Mint	Thistle, Milk
Beet	Dill	* Nepp	Thyme
* Betony	* Dittander	* Nettle, Red	* Valerian
Borage	Fennel	* Oculus Christi	* Violet
Cabbage	* Good King Henry	Orach	* Wood sorrel
Caraway	* Hartstongue	Parsley	(Onions)
Chervil	* Langdebeef	Patience	* (Sowthistle)
Chives	Leek	Pepperwort	

Herbs for sauce

* Dittander	Parsley	* (Garlic mustard)
* Hartstongue	* Pellitory	* (Wood sorrel)
Masterwort	* Sorrel	
* Mints	* Violet	

Herbs for the cup (for infusing in water or wine)

Carnation	Endive	Rosemary
Clary	Hyssop	Rue
Cost	Marjoram	* (Camomile)
Costmary	Marigold, Pot	* (Horehound)

Herbs for salad

* Alexanders	* Cress, French	* Mints	Rampion
Borage	* Daisies	* Nettle, Red Dead	* Ramsoms
* Calamint	* Dandelion	Parsley	Rocket
* Chickweed	Fennel	* Primrose buds	* Violets
Chives	* Heartsease	Purslane	* (Burnet)
			* (Cresses)

Herbs to distil

* Betony	Hyssop	Sage
Dragons	* Mugwort	* Scabious
Endive	Rose, Red	* Silverweed
* Eyebright	Rosemary	* Water Pepper
		Wormwood

Roots and bulbs

Carrots	Saffron
* Eryngo	Turnips
Parsnips	(Onions)
Radish	

Herbs for both savour and beauty (i.e. taste and/or scent)

Basil	Dill	Marjoram, Sweet	* Solomon's Seal
Carnation	Garlic	Melons	* Vervain
* Dropwort	Germander	Poppy, Garden	(Wallflower)

Also for a herber or ornamental garden

Trees	*Shrubs*	*Herbaceous plants*	
Almond	Gooseberry	Campion	Lilies
Baytree	Gourds	Columbine	Peony, Roman
Peach	Roses, White	Cornflower?	Safflower?
Pine	Vine	Hellebore	
Plum			

Additional plants also listed in the original Fromond list but not included in categories of use by the author

Anise	Fenugreek	Mandrake	Savory
* Archangel	* Gromwell	* Pennyroyal	* Smallage
* Bugle	* Herb-Ive	Poppy, White	Southernwood
Cucumber	* Henbane	Quince	* Tansy
Elecampane	Lovage	* Setterwort	Wormseed

ADDITIONAL COMMONLY GROWN PLANTS LISTED BY JON GARDENER *c.* 1350
(identified by Harvey, 1985)

Primarily aesthetically appealing plants

* Cowslip
* Daffodil
* Foxglove
  Hollyhock
  Irises
  Lavender
* Periwinkle
* Strawberry
* Tutsan
* Waterlily
* Woodruff

Primarily medicinal herbs

* Centaury
* Comfrey
  Feverfew
* Herb Robert
* Mouse-ear
* Orpine
* Polypody
* Pimpernel
* Plantains
* Yarrow

ADDITIONAL PLANTS GROWN IN ENGLISH MEDIEVAL GARDENS IN THE
WIDEST SENSE, TAKEN FROM A VARIETY OF SOURCES

Additional aesthetically appealing plants

* Lily of the Valley
  Rocket, Sweet
  Stocks

Additional culinary plants

Bean, Broad
Mustard
Parsnip
Pea
Skirrets

Orchard and nut trees

Apple varieties
Cherry, Sweet and Sour
Chestnut (Spanish)
Fig
* Hazel

Medlar
Mulberry
Pear varieties
Service
Walnut

Native hedging and woodland trees and shrubs

Alder	Ivy
Ash	Holly
Birch	Maple
Bramble	Oak
Elm	Roses: R. rubiginosa,
Hazel	R. pimpinellifolia
Hawthorn	Willows

Useful native additions for present-day re-creations

Bluebell	Fern, female and male
Broom	Guelder rose
Celandine, Greater	Origan (wild marjoram)
Corncockle	Strawberry, Wild
Corn marigold	Thyme, Creeping
Cowslip	

Other native plants if justifiable. A wide range of turf plants.

Plants in Medieval Medicine

Although we tend to be sceptical about medieval herbal medicine, little do we realise how much our present-day health is based on medieval practices. In Western medicine we still use the pre-Christian Hippocratic ethics, adopted in Europe in medieval times; we live predominantly on plants, and treat our diseases with their derivatives. Medieval precepts conducive to health, both then and now, were laid down in the tenth century and they recommended good air, exercise and rest, and moderation (not abstention) in all the feelings of joy, anger, fear and distress. This holistic attitude to medicine continued well into the nineteenth century, when it was replaced by faith in drugs and surgery, and it is only now coming to prominence again.

In our quest for the medical components of medieval gardens at different levels of society our knowledge is so limited that we can only feel our way in the dark by pondering on particular cases. The wealthy John Arderne, physician to John of Gaunt, discoursed on medical ethics: 'Know ye that it is not required that all these at once and together be used ... but know this, that to worthy and noble men it is seemly to put more noble medicines and more dear.' A nice example of this principle is shown in the correspondence of Wibald, abbot successively of monasteries in Belgium, Germany and

A selection of leaves and flowers from the Fromond utilitarian list.

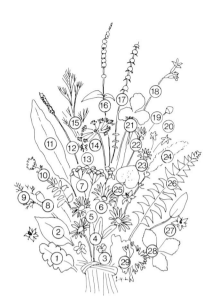

Key for plants from the Fromond list. 1. Betony; 2. Bay; 3. Heartsease; 4. Sage; 5. Ox-eye daisy; 6. Pot marigold; 7. Tansy; 8. Poppy; 9. Fennel; 10. Wild marjoram; 11. Hartstongue fern; 12. Lavender; 13. Germander; 14. Fennel; 15. Southernwood; 16. Mint; 17. Pennyroyal; 18. Rocket; 19. Camomile; 20. Sweet violet; 21. Avens; 22. Chives; 23. Camomile; 24. Hyssop; 25. Violet; 26. Polypody fern; 27. Borage; 28. Strawberry; 29. Wormwood.

Italy. Writing to a friend with a cold, in November 1147, he said: 'We send you an antidote. It will however be a *diacalamentis* which, though cheap, has the same effectiveness as *diamargariton*'. The former contained the garden plants catmint, parsley, lovage, celery, pennyroyal, wild thyme, and fennel – all hot and dry in the second degree, to counteract the cold and moist phlegmatic symptoms. The latter remedy contained the exotic powder of pearl and ivory, and expensive hot, dry spices – cloves, cinnamon, galingale, aloes, nutmeg, ginger, and camphor – obtainable from apothecaries. Abbot Wibald knew that he did not need to impress a friend! (Opsomer-Halleux, 1986.)

Apothecaries' medicine would be backed up with prescriptions for the household to make up, such as pottage ingredients selected to suit the illness, a tisane or infusion for headaches or congestion, a fresh salad and so on. The particular establishment, whether a royal garden, infirmary, hospital or patient's own garden, would have a range of these to hand, and one could well read the 'Fromond' list as a medical one. Kymer, physician to Humphrey, Duke of Gloucester gave a list of twenty similar herbs as a medicinal pottage.

In a holistic way gardens of the wealthy were understood to aid health, as illustrated by John Malverne, Bishop Physician to Henry VI, who said that as an anti-plague aid the house air should be filled with the scent of roses, violets, bay leaves, fennel, mint and other aromatics. Even at a humble level this was implied since Chaucer mentions the flower-bedecked lodgings of Nicholas the Clerk at Oxford. The garden too would be understood to act as a *cordon sanitaire* and in fact Crescenzi, in the siting of gardens, quotes the famous tenth-century Arab physician Avicenna and his emphasis on a balance between drying fresh winds and the moisture from lakes and rivers.

In a fifteenth-century manuscript an author-physician made notes on a particular case of a woman who was presumably fairly wealthy since 'all the leeches of London' could not cure her, and who had treated herself 'through her own wit' (Rowland, 1981):

She took watercress a handful; sowthistles and fen sowthistles, wild sage, parsley, betonie, millefoyyle, golds, of each a 6th part of a handful, and she made her worts and ate it green [raw] as much as ever she must, nine times a night or ten times a day. And if she must drynk, she drank this following ptysan – she took a dyshe of barley, of wormwood, golds [marigolds], wild sage, sowthistle, roots of Alexanders, parsley, anyseed, fennel, chicory and boiled all these in three gallons of clear water till half boiled away.

The patient must have had these ingredients available in her garden, though many of them could also be found in the countryside.

Somewhere in its many gardens the monastery would grow the medicinal plants needed for ordinary medicine, including the treatment of patients *in extremis*, who, in addition to prayer, might need narcotics such as mandrake, hemlock, henbane and opium. A cache of 574 seeds of these corresponding to a known recipe, and probably surviving as a single medical preparation, has been found in the hospital refuse at Soutra on Lammermoor. But for the regular intake of monks who had been bled about six times a year, certain plants were necessary; for instance the ingredients of the first post-bloodletting drinks, according to prescribed principles, were salt water and sage, both fluid-retaining, and iron-rich parsley. If the arm had become inflamed through bloodletting the instructions were to drink hartstongue, and make a hot poultice thus: 'Take groundsel, leeks, chickweed, mint, mugwort, monk's patience, parsley. Stamp and heat in their own juice, and make a plaster' (Dawson, 1934). The infirmary garden is further discussed by John Harvey (1993), and a twelfth-century list is planted in Brother Cadfael's physic garden.

Apart from passing on such instructions as were given by doctors, the most significant progress in medicine for women came about with the de-latinising of prescriptions, since women could then grow and use many of the ingredients themselves. Margaret Paston, of the fifteenth-century Norfolk gentry family, and her daughter-in-law Margery were fine examples of women who benefited by reading the set recipes for given ailments, growing the plants and preparing them. They could do this without any medical reasoning, from at least two known books of physic that were copied in English for Margaret's husband John, by an unlettered clerk. The latter had to beg for his 20d payment for the copying (Virgoe, 1989). These ladies, who were wealthy although not aristocratic, reveal in their correspondence an adroitness in medicine, for example in a letter of 1464 from Margaret to her husband: 'Beware what medicines you take of any physicians in London …. I shall never trust them because of [the death of] your father and my uncle.' In a letter of 1473, to her chaplain at another manor, regarding a sick cousin, Margaret writes: 'give him any of my waters or other that may do him comfort. I remember that the water of mints, or other of millefleurs would be good. Send to Dame Calthorpe, she has other waters'.

In 1490 John wrote to Margery Paston asking for her poultice of 'flower of ointments', for the King's Attorney, who had a painful knee: ' But when you send the poultice you must write how it should be laid, how long without removal, whether he must wrap any more cloths about it to keep the plaster warm'. Such a poultice might be made of rue and lovage pounded with preservative honey, and perhaps a mineral powder, and applied hot.

These women gained some of their knowledge from the network of their

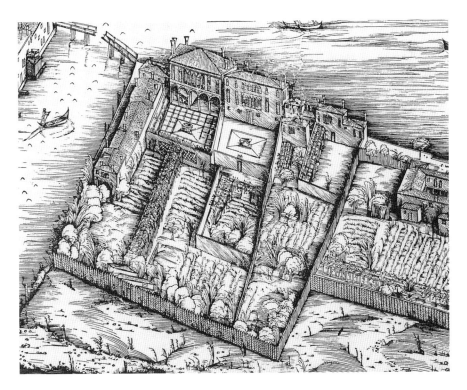

Urban-style gardens in Venice. In each the more formal herber with patterned lawns is partitioned off from an area of rougher parallel beds which represent the kitchen garden. Arbours take up less space than shade trees in cramped plots. The gardens of the Paris Goodman could have resembled these. Italian, 1500.

friends, who at various times had called in physicians. A friend of Margaret Paston wrote to her, thus: 'Mistress, my lady sent to Cambridge for a doctor of physic. If ye will anything with him he shall abide this day and the morrow. He is a right cunning man and gentle'. Such a doctor might well prescribe say a 'Genoa treacle', of Arabic origin bought dear in London, but also salads, pottages and tisanes made with the ingredients he would expect to find growing in their gardens. It seems reasonable that this advice might then be given by Margaret, to the *famuli* or servants, and their village relatives.

Eighty years earlier in about 1393 the fifteen-year-old wife of the Goodman of Paris was limited to the knowledge imparted by her husband – a few simple pottages and tisanes, the dried spice element of which revealed the Arab influence. But he explains to her how to distil without an alembic, and she, like the Paston women, could have made her 'mel roset' from 1 lb of rose petals to every 8 lbs of honey; water for the finger bowls from infused sage, rosemary and bay leaves; and other sweet waters with plants and honey from her own garden (Power, 1928; Brereton, 1981). Here then we have women who were well-read in medicine, intelligent, critical, knowing their limits in buying some medicines and making others from their own garden plants, caring of relatives and manorial or parish peasants, and whose knowledge was widely respected. Amongst the peasantry, however, apart from charms, farmyard ingredients were available, and at worst these alone without any herbal addition would suffice. Eggwhite was a styptic, pig's grease an ointment base, 'May butter' for burns, and barley meal for poultices. Further, not only at worst, but in fact then recognised as the more potent form, many plants could be collected from the wild, as asterisked in the 'Fromond' list, particularly if a peasant was instructed by the lady of the manor.

4 The Practice of Medieval Gardening

The Gardener and his Status

Adam toiled for his living on departing from Eden, and the spade became the symbol of the archetypal gardener. However it is pleasing that by the seventh century, Adam's curse had become a virtue in the eyes of the Church in the beatification of St Fiacre, one of the patron saints of gardeners. When he was offered all the land he could turn over in one day for a monastery, he succeeded in digging the boundary of a nine-acre plot.

Words such as gardener, *ortolanus*, *hortolanus*, or *gardinarius*, which were used in manuscripts, all distinguish the gardener from Langland's common labourer, 'Davy, the ditcher and delver'. The extent to which a gardener might be involved in the many additional crafts exhibited in a garden would depend upon the wealth of its owner. In a simple garden the gardener himself would construct pole trellises and tunnels tied with withies, make a plank bridge with a fork-supported hand rail, or construct a turf seat. At the other extreme in a royal garden many craftsmen with their own specialist tools would be employed, supervised by a head keeper or gardener, just as in 1986 several specialists were involved in the reconstruction of the thirteenth-century royal Queen Eleanor's Garden (p. 120).

Sometimes gardeners with particular skills came from abroad, their names being suggestive of their origin, such as Gascoigne, or Florentyn who directed the Queen's garden works at Guildford castle (Colvin, 1963). A Provençal gardener was employed in England by Queen Eleanor of Provence, and Queen Eleanor of Castile left money in her will for her Aragonese gardeners to return to Spain (Harvey, 1981). At Stirling Castle in 1509 we read: 'Item, tools for the French gardener'. Other specialists were employed temporarily, as at the Manor of Cuxham, where the recording of an isolated expense of 1d. for a gardener in connection with vine-pruning implied only half a day's work. Amongst a fine list of some eighty named gardeners Salomon is quoted, who was garden keeper to

Labours of the months, together with all parts of a nobleman's estate distilled into one illustration. *January*, feasting indoors; *February*, ploughing the fallow fields; *March*, digging the beds; *April*, picking flowers on a flowery mead; *May*, holiday; *June*, sheep-shearing; *July*, mowing the hay meadow; *August*, scything the cornfields; *September*, fruit-gathering in the fenced orchard; *October*, harvesting grapes from trellises; *November*, killing the hobbled cow; *December*, axing wood in the copse. A late 15th-century Flemish illustration for Crescenzi's MS of 1305.

Henry I, his son Ralph keeper to Henry II and *his* son Geoffrey keeper to Richard I and King John – a family training over some seventy years. This implies both a pride in the craft and a continuity in gardening practices (Harvey, 1981).

In the instruction laid down by St Benedict in his *Rule*, prayer was balanced both by intellectual study and physical work, including gardening. By the twelfth century, however, the Benedictine monasteries were well on the way to a less physically orientated way of life, and lay gardeners were brought in. The later Cistercian movement counteracted this trend, with a concentration on horticulture and agriculture at the very fringes of inhabitable land. But even here there developed a dichotomy between non-labouring choir monks and the labouring *conversi* or lay brothers, as monks became increasingly drawn from the esquire level of society. The monastic *ortolanus* was the obedientiary or official who had administrative charge of the gardens, arranging and paying for the labour and keeping records such as those found in the monastic accounts for Norwich: 'Stipend of Ralph Brenetour and others working upon the bank and cleaning the ditch in the meadow for 12 days, by the day 8d … for labourers in extracting moss from the cloister green, 6d … for grafting, 4d … for planting garlic and beans and for weeding, 2s'. There were extra items for the gardeners employed, such as their medicines, gloves, boots and repair of boots (Amherst, 1896). Sometimes other obedientiaries such as the sacrist had their own gardens, but these would usually have been tended by lay servants.

Although there are few records of named women gardeners they had their place, as for instance St Dorothy of the Cherries, and St Gertrude, both German garden saints. However women are frequently mentioned as labourers, weeding, harvesting, loading manure and gathering fruit, and it was common for women to be employed as bean-planters at an unchanged rate of a quarter acre per day for 1d throughout the Middle Ages. This is not to say that women were bereft of design or garden skills. We know of several English queens, such as the Eleanors of Provence and Castile, and Philippa of Hainault, and suspect more, who had strong interests in gardening. In the ecclesiastical world too, where many abbots, priors, and bishops did so much for agriculture and horticulture the Abbess Euphemia of Wherwell Abbey is notable. Outside the infirmary chapel, 'she enclosed a large space which was adorned on the northside with pleasant vines and trees … by the riverside she built various offices, a space being left in the centre where nuns are able to enjoy the pure air …. She surrounded the court with a wall and round it made gardens and vineyards and shrubberies in places that were formerly useless and barren' (*Victorian County History: Berkshire*, II, p.132).

With the emergence of a prosperous yeomanry in and before the sixteenth cen-

St Fiacre, a patron saint of gardeners, with Bible and spade. A 15th-century alabaster statue, 11 in high.

tury, the housewife became mistress of her own garden. Master Fitzherbert in 1538 in *The Booke of Husbandry*, after 40 years' experience as a householder, writes, 'And at the beginning of March or a little before, is time for a wife to make her garden and to get as many good seeds as she can'. Again with the new *bourgeoisie* we find the young wife of the Goodman of Paris, in about 1393, being instructed in the art of gardening, in order that she herself could be the supervisor rather than the labouring gardener, instructing her *famuli* to 'plant wet, sow dry'.

Principles of Measurement and Layout

Parts of the human body are as good a unit of measurement for gardeners today as they were in the Middle Ages – a foot, a step (of about two and a half feet) and the same in forward reach. A hand-span of eight or nine inches gave a suitable distance for planting leeks, as it still does, and a hand or palm width still measures our horses. Surely the quaintest measure is in the ninth-century Irish instruction for making a wattle fence: 'It is to be twelve hands high [36–8 inches]. There are to be three bands of wattle on it, one at the top, one in the middle, one along the base. Each post is pushed down by hand into the ground, and struck three blows with a mallet. The length of a foot as far as the big toe is to be left between every two posts. Each post is to be three hands high above the top band of wattle, and there is to be a blackthorn crest on the fence.' For soft and long and curved measures, the arm span of about six feet or a fathom, was useful for measuring the girth of a tree, or several linked arm spans for measuring bean stacks in a yard. Even in 1986 the whole human form was the basis for designing the shape of a tunnel arbour at Queen Eleanor's Garden, Winchester.

In England the foot was standardised to its present length in the reign of Henry I (1100–1135) and the measured acre became 66 by 660 feet in the reign of Edward I (1272–1307) based on an original principle of thirty-three turns of the plough, forwards and back again. The standard perch of 16½ square feet was a subdivision of the measured acre. These measures were no doubt crude in practice but were important for calculating the seed required, the yield to be accounted, labour to be paid, and boundaries to be measured.

With so many perches in use ranging between 16, 16½, 18, 20 and 22 feet, and the 'church' pole of 21 feet, consistency had to be maintained at a local level. There is a European tradition that in each parish the feet of the first sixteen men leaving the church were measured. A wealthy English landowner, Henry de Bray, in 1292, cannot have been the only person to have recorded the local perch as 'sixteen feet as measured on the chapel at Harlestone'.

Another Roman measure of twelve feet, which was based on two arm spans,

The sophisticated Burgundian influence. Beds show corner and dot plants of roses, pinks, etc, together with geometric planting patterns for low herbs. Trellised bed edges maintain the neat pattern, but there is no attempt at an overall effect as in 16th- and 17th-century gardens. French *c.*1470

divided in halves, then quarters, and then into eighths to give a unit of 1½ feet, was sometimes used in architecture, for instance at Charlemagne's Palace at Aachen. The Roman measuring rod of ten feet together with an associated cord, was frequently used also, and again rather than being divided into feet it could be halved, quartered and then divided into eighths, relating to the Roman pace, step, and *pedipassus* of 5 feet, 2½ feet and 1¼ feet respectively. It was on this basis that the idealised plan of St Gall was imaginatively deciphered (Horn & Born, 1979). The measure of 2½ feet was used by John Rea as late as the seventeenth century for laying out parterres, and the Oxford Botanic garden was based on a ten-foot scale as late as the seventeenth century.

Plots needed reliable right-angled sides particularly for vegetables grown in rows, and although the average peasant might have a rough go, the sophisticated garden architect who was laying out regular square beds would have to measure more accurately. Indeed geometry, literally 'measurement of the earth', sprang from the necessity continually to re-lay the agricultural plots of the ancient Egyptian Nile flood plain. Out of this came Euclid's three:four:five ratio for constructing a right-angle which was carried out in practice by cords knotted in those proportions, and the Egyptian word for surveyor meant 'knotted rope bearer.' Only two records of measured cord lengths are known, one being quoted by Richard Benyse in 1520 who referred to a cord of 82½ feet, waxed against shrinkage. This measurement is not so surprising since it is five perches, or a furlong, and equalling an eighth of an acre length, and even today corporation allotments are still allocated in areas of perches. The second

Harvesting leeks from a bed. Three rows of leeks are seen, and the bed is probably about 4ft wide, narrow enough to reach across. The leeks appear to be planted sloping, as suggested by Albertus Magnus. Note the multi-purpose mattock-type tool. German, 15th century, illustrating Crescenzi's text.

cord was given to the gardener at Winchester College in 1437 and was a very expensive one amongst other cheap examples. It was fourteen fathoms long, and equivalent to a labourer's wages for two weeks. Why fourteen fathoms, or eighty-four feet? Out of this length a three:four:five triangle could be made, twenty-one, twenty-eight and thirty-five feet. A European medieval horticultural unit of twenty-one feet could also be laid out by the triangular method using such an eighty-four-foot cord, as illustrated on p. 16.

The St Gall Plan is the only extant measurable medieval plan, and modules of 1¼ feet were used here, but the plan is in addition resplendent with number symbolism. There is much discussion about the danger of reading too much into the meaning of numbers, but it was a subject which fascinated the medieval mind, and both the St Gall plan and the monastic buildings of Cluny indisputably show evidence of playing with numbers. According to the seventh-century Spanish encyclopaedist, St Isidore, a 'perfect' number equals the sum of all its sub-multiples. There were only three perfect numbers, 6, 28 and 496, together with 1 which had its own perfection. To extend Isidore's observations further it can be seen that the perfect numbers 1, 6 and 28 (=35), and all their sub-multiples 2, 3, 4, 7 and 14, are all contained within the number 84, the same number of feet of cord used to lay out the 21-foot square. This would indeed seem to make a 'perfect' garden cord!

The medieval gardener had a great degree of freedom in measuring, or not measuring his plots. It is necessary for us to remember this since, apart from the St Gall plan, which was never actually constructed, there is no medieval documentary evidence, other than illustrations, for the widths of garden beds and paths. The medieval gardener would have been aware of the Roman principle, quoted also in the post-medieval treatise *The Gardeners Labyrinth* written in 1594, that 'beds should be so contrived that the hands of those who weed them may easily reach the middle of their breadth, so that those who are weeding may not be forced to tread on seedlings, to the help of which let the paths be of such a width (as a man's foot) that they may weed first one half and then the other half of the bed'. Furthermore if there is room to kneel on a wider path, and the gardener supports himself on one hand as is sometimes illustrated, then plant beds can be as much as five feet wide. The associated 3¾ foot paths of the ideal St Gall monastery would in fact allow one man to walk past another kneeling man. We can see that this gives a practical basis for the working gardener, and for re-creating gardens today. The more precise and geometric principles in the layouts of later gardens remain undiscovered but must be the result of a wide range of cultural influences, not only based on the practical concerns of gardening as a craft, but on higher goals which elevated gardens to an art form. Nowadays in archaeological work the metric system is necessary for

Making a timber-framed bench. The box was filled with rubble and then turfed or filled with soil if roses or flowers were planted in it rather than behind it. 15th century.

A pair of gloves or mittens. Three-fingered weeding gloves were used for weeding thistles and the like; they were also used by shepherds, and perhaps by masons. From a French misericord carving, 15th century.

accurate recording, but it is meaningless as an interpretive tool, since it is one ten-millionth of a quadrant of the meridian, which would certainly confuse not only our medieval gardener, and mathematical abbot, but also the present-day craftsman and re-creator of medieval gardens.

Tools and Ingenious Devices

Manuscript depictions of gardeners' tools give clues to the kind of work which was carried out in a medieval garden. The design of individual tools varied throughout Europe, as it still does today. In England alone, for example, there are twenty-five regional types of billhook still in use.

The medieval spade was either one- or two-sided, fashioned from a single piece of straight-grained wood with a T-handle added, and it was commonly 'shoed' with iron, nailed on at the sides. The mattock is rarely seen today except in peasant communities, but was and is a useful multipurpose tool for digging trenches, breaking up soil, rooting up unwanted shrubs and roots, and surface hoeing. The billhook was necessary for pruning, making and laying of hedges, 'shredding' or cleaning up trunk sides for fuel, coppicing, and any jobs in the lord's wood covered by the legal term 'by hook and by crook'. The sickle, sometimes with a serrated edge, was used mainly for cutting crops, such as corn or beans, but was also useful for trimming grass round tree trunks, stream sides or paths. The scythe was necessary for mowing the valuable water meadows, or any odd strips of ground. Orchard grass, if mowed twice annually, yielded an aesthetically appealing turf, a method still advocated by Christopher Lloyd for twentieth-century orchards, in order to create a 'flowery mead'. As late as the turn of this century one Scottish bowling club green was still cut by scythe, so we can assume that a very fine effect could have been achieved in the main cloister of a monastery. Forks and rakes were used for dung, and for collecting and turning the hay, and William Fitzherbert describes the process of cutting the wood for making such tools in the autumn: 'when the housebonde sytteth by the fyre, and hath nothing to do then may he make [the rake teeth] ready and bore the holes with his wymble and drive them fast and hard and wedge them with oke'.

Apart from using the mattock, weeding was done with a weeding hook and forked stick. Some of the plants we call weeds were actually eaten, but the main medieval weeds, as defined by Fitzherbert and Tusser, were docks, stinking mayweed, cleavers, thistles, knapweed, corncockle, cornflower, and charlock. Many of these are what we delight in calling 'wild flowers' but Miriam Rothschild's 'Farmers' Nightmare,' better implies the damage done by the smothering of crops and blunting of sickles! Here is a description of weeding (Fitzherbert, 1534):

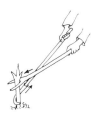

Weeding with a hook and a fork

A clay watering pot

Watering device of the Goodman of Paris

Use of forked branches

Then must ye have a wedynge-hoke with a socket, set upon a little staffe a yard longe, and this hoke wolde be … grounde sharpe, both behind and before. In his other hand he hath a forked stycke a yarde longe, and with his forked stycke he putteth the weed from him, and he putteth the hoke beyond the root of the wede, and putteth it to him, and cutteth the weed fast by the earth.

Amongst other implements were axes of various forms, the vital gardener's knife, a trio of grafting tools – small saw, wedge knife and grafting knife – baskets, mallets or beetles, ladders, iron crowbars, dibbles, seed sowing box, sieves, spring shears of the sheep-shearing type, rods and knotted measuring lines. The unique find of a turf cutter of modern design must have delighted the archeologists at Weoley Castle. Implements which we consider indispensable but which we never read about in medieval times included a little hand fork and trowel, the four-pronged fork, and hoe of the pushing type. The first illustration of a wheelbarrow of a modern design is fifteenth-century (Harvey, 1981, fig. 35), the more usual medieval design being flat. The gardener's apron with the corners held up became a tool for gathering. Gloves were worn for rough work such as thistle-weeding, clearing brambles and mattocking, and an intriguing three-fingered variety is clearly illustrated in the Holkham Bible picture book, though they may have also been used by other craftsmen, such as masons or shepherds. For most tasks, as with the twentieth-century gardener, the hands were uncluttered by gloves.

Many ingenious devices were employed. The simple tree-fork was put to many uses, such as the carrying of loads of rods or supporting the cane trellises used to cover flower beds. Gourd-shaped clay watering pots were operated on the same principle as metal ones in wealthy households (Moorhouse, 1991). These had a single hole at the top for filling and ten or twelve holes at the bottom from which water sprayed out. The flow could be stopped by placing the thumb over the top hole. One of the most ingenious ideas is the using of a cow-horn funnel to compress and twist the straw rope from which bee skeps were made, used together with a channelled bone, through which a tying strand of bramble was threaded (see p. 44). Cane and metal frames were used to support carnations and lilies in pots, those with vertical sides being placed in holes in the pot rim. Alternatively, a bucket-shape arose by pushing canes into the perimeter soil of sloping-sided pots. Metal 'wheels' were later used to form tiered topiary shapes of cypress, pomegranate and box. Even a moral approach to weeding was used by a tenth-century monk who crucified his weeds on a cross of strings over the garden, 'whereon in summertime he hung them, stretching out their roots against the heat of the sun, that they might never live again'!

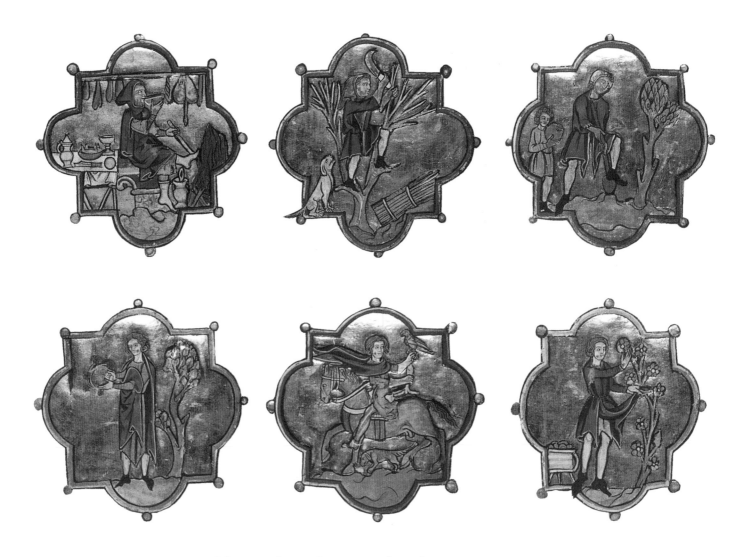

The Occupations of the Months – The Seasonal Setting

One of the delights of medieval manuscripts is the variety of ways in which the occupations of the seasons are depicted, with the main theme following a set pattern throughout the period. Whilst there is an ingenuity in a fifteenth-century illustration which contracts all the occupations of the months and the whole of an estate into one illustration, the more common form of thirteenth- and fourteenth-century calendars is a set of twelve miniatures which show a happy

Occupations of the months. The monthly initials of a calendar of Saints' Days in a late 13th-century Book of Hours, Lièges. *January*, feasting; *February*, pruning; *March*, digging; *April*, giving; *May*, enjoying; *June*, picking roses;

(*Occupations of the months*, cont.) *July*, mowing; *August*, reaping; *September*, bargaining; *October*, tramping grapes; *November*, fattening pigs; *December*, killing the ox.

worker in an ordered society. Like misericord art there is a simplicity combined with humour or sharp observation which is lost in the later more elaborate calendars. At the date of the calendar illustrated above, which was painted in Lièges around 1280, the agriculture-based society was at its optimum.

January shows the last of the feasting, before spring ploughing starts after Candlemas. Sausages, rope, and game-birds hang to dry or to be smoked from the rafters above a laden table. A small mammal, perhaps a hedgehog or suckling pig, awaits the diner who indulgently warms his foot, dries his boot and heats his 'mulled wine' or Ypocras, whilst drinking. *February* is the pruning month. 'The pruner perched amid the trees may sing', wrote Columella in *c.* AD 300 and here the dog seems to accompany the song. The hazel underwood is coppiced for fuel with its straight rods making neat bundles or 'bavins' for the long manor bread-ovens. *March* is the month for digging, not only garden beds but in the orchard and vineyard around each tree, a process known as ablaqueation or root-pruning, with the addition of fresh soil.

April is the month of giving, in which nature gives to man through the garden and countryside, and lovers give to each other. *May* is a time for holiday, before the hectic months from June to September. Here the rustic pleasure of the peasant, hawking foot-loose and fancy free with gown flowing (forwards!) in the wind, contrasts with the artificial code of chivalry. *June* is often shown as the sheep-shearing or weeding month, but here the gardener collects the red roses of Provence, *Rosa gallica*, into his 'lap' or apron and then into a three-legged container. These would be used for oil of roses, a gentle soother of chapped skin, or for garlands.

In *July* every spare corner was mown, whether peasant's garden or lord's orchard (as suggested by the tree) or the water meadows fringed with willows. A sharpening hone is attached to the scythe handle, and the ale jug hangs on the forked branch. *August* is the reaping month, and here the man cuts high to leave valuable stubble for other purposes whilst the woman binds the sheaf and the hawk-eyed bailiff supervises. *September* is the harvesting and accounting month, after threshing, with the new year starting at Michaelmas, 29 September. The surplus stock, possibly eggs, is offered to a tight-fisted merchant who retains his coins.

October is the wine month, and here the gathered grapes are being trampled whilst the treader tastes the partly fermented must. Or perhaps it is cider, trampled from bruised apples, since the assistant holds a container of apples. *November* is pannage month, the peasant often having the right to fatten his pig on acorn mast knocked from the lord's trees. The pig rubs against the tree trunk with a look of bliss, not aware of his December death. *December* is the culling month, and here the trusting ox is oblivious of the axe hanging over him.

Whether labourer on his own land, or employee on another's, a man's lot was completely interwoven with the estate year, and the agricultural year, his own rhythm being dictated by the natural seasons of growth, harvest and dormancy.

The Nurture of Plants

There was deep understanding of the necessity to feed plants, using dung from fallowed animals, household rubbish, marl to improve soil, or soil-rich scourings from the annual clearing of ditches. Some dovecot floors had channels leading to tanks so that liquid manure could be collected after cleaning out, as well as using the dry dung, and Palladius also mentions the collection of liquid manure from compost heaps. One tiny manuscript painting of only 2 x 3 inches shows a vine being pruned and the prunings being burnt in a flaming bonfire beside it. The potassium-rich ash is still returned to the ground from mobile bonfires in wheelbarrows after pruning in the vineyards of Provence.

The concept of rotation of field crops was understood, including the beneficial effect of buying in of agricultural seed from other land, with garden seed exchange even amongst housewives being advocated for the same reason (Tusser, 1580):

> Good housewife in summer will save her own seeds
> Against the next year as occasion needs
> One seed for another to make an exchange
> With fellowly neighbourhood seemeth not strange

Many forms of propagation were used. Trees were grown from nuts, acorns, pips and stones. Particular types of apples and pears were propagated by grafting on to saplings or rooted suckers of wild forms, since fruit varieties do not grow true to type from pips. Regarding herbaceous propagation it was advised to 'sow dry, set [plant] wet'. Seed was obtained by careful shaking of seedheads onto canvas cloths, and then dried in a sun-warmed room, and kept in leather bags or wooden boxes. Layering is not often mentioned, but was certainly used for vine layering, a vine shoot being led through a hole in a basket which was then filled with earth, and left a while, as described by the Roman Columella, but also illustrated in the fifteenth century (see p. 87). Other plants and shrubs such as vines, roses and rosemary (the 'husband' of lavender) were propagated by cuttings, the latter even transported encased in wax to prevent drying out. Yet other plants, particularly herbs, were split for their own good, as described by Walahfrid Strabo (Payne, 1966):

> But within itself is the germ of civil war;
> For unless the new growth is cut away, it turns
> Savagely on its parent and chokes to death
> The older stems in bitter jealousy

Transplanting of leeks and some forms of onions was also undertaken, and of brassicas when about four weeks old, these and seedlings being very carefully watered, according to Walahfrid, by trickling it through the fingers. Although little was written about weeds and pests in medieval times, much of the fuller instructions of the classical writers would have been passed down through the generations. Pests such as ants and caterpillars were a problem, and appropriate advice is given

Grafting

by the Goodman of Paris to his young wife. Sawdust round ants' nests is suggested, and caterpillar eggs should be looked for under the leaves, those leaves being then cut off. The attitude to earthworms was more ambiguous and we find the franklin gardener in the anonymous *Mum and the Sothseggar* giving his personal view:

> And I wrought up the weeds that worren my plants;
> And wormes that worken not, but waster my herbes,
> I dash them to death, and delve out their dennes.

Weeds were of course a pest. Nettles were one of the many coarse plants which were then known as weeds, others being docks, thistles and swamping mallows. However most of the fine 'weeds' of our kitchen and herbaceous borders were considered to be food or medicine.

It was understood that to produce fruit and flowers the natural exuberance of plants had to be quelled by judicious pruning of 'superfluities'. Albertus Magnus prescribes this for trees, and Bartholomew recommends it for vines and roses, giving careful instructions that the cut surface should slope downwards so that rain-drops will fall off the tips. Such pruning and also shaping for aesthetic reasons reached the limits in medieval topiary in the form of a tiered 'estrade' or cake-stand shape. The production of fine lawns by reducing the natural exuberance of grass by frequent scything and beating down has already been described.

Rather than pruning back, some plants needed gentle support by staking, such as newly planted trees. Alder poles were necessary for supporting vines, brushwood for peas and floppy herbs, and forked sticks for the valuable seedheads of leek and onions. Roses were tied to trellises and arbours, our present-day bass being available even then. There were various forms of support for the long stalks of lilies and carnations, and one composed of horizontal trelliswork over a bed could presumably be raised as the plants grew, still having its wire counterpart in the greenhouses of present-day carnation growers (see p. 100).

An orchard, showing newly grafted and 'bandaged' trees. Flemish, 15th century.

Making hay at the river's edge. A peasant sharpens his scythe, his pottle of ale nearby. The osiers supply rods and withies. The following quotation, originally recorded in 1324, is illustrated (J. Z. Titow): 'Elyas Oueryegat … with his congenors shall spread the grass after the meadows are mowed, and lift, make and stack hay thereof and shall receive nothing for this work … the lord providing food once a day worth 1½d.' Italian 15th century.

The different types of planting are explored in the following pages, but to summarise, trees and shrubs were grown in orchards, and as isolated plants and hedges, with roses and vines on trellises. Herbaceous plants were occasionally grown in beds at seat level, but more usually almost at ground level, in isolated beds or rudimentary herbaceous borders. Some were grown in pots, which were moved to grace a particular corner when in full flower, or to 'deck-up' houses in winter or summer. A beautiful poem written by Walahfrid Strabo in Reichenau, Germany, well over a thousand years ago encapsulates the philosophy and labour of all loving gardeners, of which the translated extract below gives a foretaste (Payne, 1966). His garden of herb beds has been re-created in Germany at Lake Constance.

> But this little patch which lies facing east
> In the small open courtyard before my door
> Was full – of nettles! All over
> My small piece of land they grew, their barbs
> Tipped with a smear of tingling poison.
> What should I do? So thick were their ranks …
>
> So I put it off no longer. I set to with my mattock
> And dug up the sluggish ground. From their embraces
>
> I tore those nettles though they grew and grew again.

Loggia opening on to enclosed garden, featuring herbaceous borders, a raised flower bed suitable also as a bench, and beds with cane plant supports. 15th century.

I destroyed the tunnels of the moles that haunt dark places,
And back to the realms of light I summoned the worms.
Then my small patch was warmed by winds from the south
And the sun's heat. That it should not be washed away,
We faced it with planks and raised it in oblong beds
A little above the level ground. With a rake
I broke the soil up bit by bit, and then
Worked in from on top the leaven of rich manure.
Some plants we grow from seed, some from old stocks
We try to bring back to the youth they knew before ….

Then come the showers of Spring, from time to time
Watering our tiny crop, and in its turn
The gentle moon caresses the delicate leaves ….

5 *Medieval Gardens Re-Created*

The Shrewsbury Quest Monastic Garden

Shrewsbury has become a centre of pilgrimage for those who know Brother Cadfael, the fictitious twelfth-century herbalist monk chronicled by Ellis Peters. To bring to life the monastic scene associated with him, the Shrewsbury Quest was established in 1994 on a plot of previously derelict land at the Abbey Foregate adjacent to the abbey, now ringed by a newly constructed perimeter cloister.

As we have seen, monastic gardens ranged over many acres and were of several types, yet at Shrewsbury there is only a twelfth of an acre in which to represent them. The design brief requested a physic garden, a pleasure garden and an area displaying the main utilitarian plants of a cellarer's garden. However, although we have a good idea of the plants which brought these gardens alive in Cadfael's time (*c.*1150), our knowledge of the design of such early gardens is scanty. It was therefore decided to tie the physic garden, for which we have some design clues, closely to Brother Cadfael and to link the pleasure garden to the establishment of the Great Parliament in Shrewsbury in 1398. By this time we have written evidence for pleasure garden design. The basic food and utilitarian plants typical of a cellarer's garden would be displayed in a few beds of traditional proportions. These three gardens would be linked by features typically seen in an entrance *curia*, or green court, within an abbey precinct.

The soil level of the beds was raised to comply with English Heritage and health and safety regulations. The beds are now contained by six- to eight-inch-high oak boards, one-and-a-half inches thick. Arguably, proximity to the foundations of old buildings, and a high water table (as here) caused by the nearness of a river would have been reason enough for the raising of soil in medieval gardens.

BROTHER CADFAEL'S PHYSIC GARDEN By a rare stroke of luck the plan of the Christ Church herbarium at Canterbury provided a perfect model for designing the garden (see p. 36). The spot can still be walked on today, adjacent to Canterbury Cathedral, and its size of about 30 by 50 feet is approximately that now apportioned to Cadfael at Shrewsbury. The diagonal symbol used for the fencing suggests oak lath trellis, and cloisters still run along one side. The plan also shows parallel beds of mixed-coloured plants. Care had to be taken that the present-day requirement for wheelchair access did not destroy the medieval design, paths of four feet in width being necessary to give an adequate turning circle. The problem has been solved at Shrewsbury by laying out a four-foot access path round a central block of parallel beds, the block being raised and edged with oak boards. Cadfael had occasional helpers such as Sulien Blount of Ellis Peter's *The Potter's Field*, and even today the garden helpers clad in monastic habits confirm the adequacy of the two-foot paths between the beds in the block for tending plants.

The plants were selected from researched lists such as those compiled by Aelfric, Macer and Neckam (Harvey, 1981). The English component of the Macer list compiled on the continent in the early part of the eleventh century and 'eng-lished' in the fourteenth century is particularly useful since it describes the exact ways in which these plants would have been used by a twelfth-century medical man. Further research on the Welsh physicians of the Myddfai covering the twelfth to the eighteenth century will supplement the list of plants which a Welshman such as Cadfael could have used in a town so close to Wales. The plants range from the little pretty-leaved betony or woundwort, which was used by Cadfael not only for cleansing wounds but for more purposes than any other medical plant, to the towering fennel and the woad, whose blood-clotting quality was perhaps the reason for it being prized by early warriors. A full list of plants grown in the garden is available from the Shrewsbury Quest.

It was decided not to allow the twentieth century to intrude into every corner. A small private area has been fenced off for Cadfael's use alone. Here in an arbour of vine combined with poisonous bryony his desk and stool will appear (when a donor sees fit to celebrate his memory!). He could have sat here, making notes, surrounded by his 'library' of plants. In this corner grows another poisonous plant, monkshood, which killed Gervase Bonel. There are plants with anaesthetic qualities such as mandrake and soporific plants such as poppies, with which Cadfael experimented. Irritant plants such as rue and hellebore are also fenced off. Monastic travellers exchanged plants, and new varieties might also have been safeguarded. Perhaps we can imagine that one such gift received by Cadfael was hyssop, a valuable medicinal plant, not officially recorded in England until about AD 1200.

We have in the fictitious Cadfael's garden a very clear picture of a real medieval medicine garden and the ingredients for a twelfth-century medicine chest. To share this knowledge further, labels are provided, explaining their twelfth-century medical function, mostly to alleviate symptoms rather than effect a cure. Some of the plants which are included for completeness would of course have been as readily gathered in the countryside, such as plantain, dock and mugwort.

Through re-creating such a garden it has become evident that a much larger area would be necessary to fulfil all the medical needs of any monastery, as well as the poor it served. It would seem therefore that the similar small area which existed at Christ Church, Canterbury, carefully fenced off, might have been used only for the poisonous or rare plants, or perhaps for nurturing cuttings and seedlings before transplanting.

THE ABBOT'S HERBER, 1398   From lists as early as those of Macer and Neckam (c.1200) we have a good idea of the plants growing in an early pleasure garden, but it is not until we have at least one medieval writer's description of the layout of such a garden that we can justify putting a pencil to a drawing board. The cosmopolitan pedigree of the herber described by Albertus or Crescenzi around 1285–1305 has already been mentioned (see p. 13), and the 'Square Garden of Henry the Poet', c.1300, shows that at least a simple version of the Albertus-type herber with a turf centre and four perimeter herbaceous borders already existed in England (Harvey, 1987). An interpretation of such descriptions is shown in the turf end of the illustration on p. 16.

For the abbot's garden at Shrewsbury further details have been added to this simple plan. Albertus suggests a water feature, and now at Shrewsbury crossed paths give access to a *servatorium*, or temporary fish storage pond, which authentically would have been lead-lined and slowly irrigated. Perhaps we can imagine Richard II on his historic visit to Shrewsbury presenting his most likely host the abbot with a fine breeding bream. Like those bouquets of flowers which are given on arrival to a twentieth-century hostess, immediate temporary water is needed in which to display the gift.

Shade was given by trees or by trellis-supported vines, and at Shrewsbury a

Monastic garden features at Shrewsbury Quest. (a) Brother Cadfael's 12th-century physic garden; (b) Cadfael's private garden; (c) abbot's herber; (d) cellarer's vegetable beds (one perch wide); (e) green court with tree seat; (f) Merrels game area.

A freestone fishpond of the storage type. The pond contains pike and other fish and ducks. Figures can be seen catching fish by shooting, scooping with a net, draw-netting and baiting. In the background is a park type of garden. Drawn by C. J. Bond from the Pope's Palace mural of 1343 in Avignon.

tunnel pole-arbour of semi-circular section has been incorporated, supporting vines, honeysuckle and climbing *alba* roses. In the perimeter border, we would expect a selection of plants listed up to the time of Friar Daniel *c.*1375 and Jon Gardener *c.*1400, using for guidance the thirteenth-century phrase 'every sweet-smelling herb … and likewise all sorts of flowers as violet, columbine, lily, rose and the like.' In addition to plants of Cadfael's time would be introductions from abroad, such as wallflowers, hollyhocks, lavender and hyssop.

Within a packed medieval monastic precinct a herber of such small size would have been feasible, but if space allowed it would have been supplemented by an area of beds and paths filled with aromatic herbs such as savory, origan, sage, fennel and elecampane, not only to delight the sense of smell but, according to Albertus, 'to refresh the sight and cause admiration at their many forms'.

THE CELLARER'S BEDS   At Shrewsbury there are only about one hundred square yards in which to represent the range of plants which would have been grown in a food and utilitarian garden normally spanning several acres. Traditional beds designed to be narrow enough to reach across have been built up on a central plot whose four-foot beds and two-foot paths fit into a perch width of sixteen feet. The most basic vegetables are grown here, such as coleworts, onions, leeks, leaf beet, and broad beans eaten green, to show the staple green element of the medieval diet.

Other beds have salad plants and leek and colewort seedlings for transplanting. Strewing herbs such as fennel, mints, wormwood and hyssop are also grown, as well as utilitarian plants which would normally be produced in large quantities such as flax for linen and bandages, and hemp for ropes and sacking. The three basic textile dye plants are displayed. Madder for red-browns, woad for blue, and dyer's greenweed for yellow-greens produced the complete range of colour found not only in peasant clothing, but also in the richest fifteenth-century tapestries. Bee skeps on a stand complete the scene.

An ornamental gourd-shaped water pot. The lady has just removed her thumb from the top filling hole, allowing water to fall from the lower holes on to the pinks. Pedestalled tubs were common. French tapestry, c.1400.

THE GREEN COURT, OR *CURIA* The green court of a precinct provided turf for grazing and was crossed by tracks leading to various buildings. The small piece of turf at Shrewsbury will be managed as a wild flower area, in which meadow, hedgerow and cornfield flowers will be established, as though they had encroached from the neighbouring countryside. The 'Farmer's Nightmare' seed mixture (presently available) contains such common medieval plants as cornflower, corn cockle, corn marigold and mayweed.

The black mulberry tree, symbolic of Christ's Passion, has had to be rejected for practical reasons, and instead the twice-flowering Glastonbury thorn has been chosen. This is surrounded by a periwinkle-topped tree seat supported by pole sides, such as could once have given a seat in the shade to some traveller awaiting an appointment. Carts, a wheelbarrow and garden tools of the time are dispersed around the court, amongst them a water barrel and ceramic thumb-pots for watering, with which adults as well as children enjoy assisting Cadfael!

The needs of child novices at a monastery were catered for in medieval times. Bowls, for instance, were available for them at Durham, and the lines of board games such as draughts and Fox and Geese have been found scratched on cloister benches. This has been done here at Shrewsbury, and in addition the game of Merrells has been laid out on the ground.

Dried plants and produce from the fields and gardens have been incorporated in the gatehouse, storehouse, dining hall, scriptorium and infirmary, and Cadfael's hut is festooned with drying herbs and shelved with potions, whilst the sound of doves can be heard in the rafters, awaiting Cadfael's return.

Bayleaf: A Yeoman's Homestead, c.1500

The Bayleaf farmhouse was moved from its original position before the Bough Beech Reservoir in Kent was able to submerge it for ever. It has now been reconstructed at the Weald and Downland Museum, Singleton, near Chichester, Sussex. The present farm complex, garden and associated 'History of Farming' exhibition was conceived, researched and executed under the direction of Christopher Zeuner and Richard Harris by some twenty museum staff and consultants, and was opened in 1990.

By the early fifteenth century a new agriculturally based middle class was establishing itself, for whose successors William Fitzherbert subsequently wrote an estate management book in 1534, claiming forty years' experience as an estate manager and householder. Later in the century, Thomas Tusser produced his own rhymed doggerel advice, perhaps the worst lines being: 'For things of the bod, forgive us oh God'! The texts of these two writers in particular described rural habits in detail which had been largely unrecorded for hundreds of years, providing a rich source for present-day re-creation at this level of society. Although these new yeomen built themselves elaborate timber-framed houses, the holdings themselves remained mainly utilitarian. In fact, even a small manor *curia* 'farmed' out to a tenant, or only rarely visited by the lord, resembled this re-created yeoman homestead. A fishpond or a wider than usual water-filled perimeter ditch containing fish would be chosen as a status symbol in preference to an ornamental garden. Such a yeoman's property might have developed from the amalgamation of several village plots after dereliction caused by the plague in the fourteenth century, or desertion in the fifteenth. Alternatively, as in the case of Bayleaf in its original position, the property could have been an isolated farmstead. Boundaries such as 'shaws' (strips of woodland), hawthorn hedges and wattle fences demarked such properties from their surroundings, and these have been re-created at the present Bayleaf homestead, surrounding the farmyard, orchard and garden.

THE BAYLEAF SHAW 'Shaws', some thirty- to forty-feet wide, surrounded the small four- to six-acre fields, and also protected timber-framed houses. This was in direct contrast to the huge arid 'open' countryside fields, where there was hardly a tree in sight, as for instance at Cuxham (p. 32). Contrary to our vision of the 'ancient' woodland of the Middle Ages, most woods were of this managed shaw or coppice type (Rackham, 1986). We are only now beginning to value again the immense renewable energy, which we term 'bio-mass', contained in these coppices, the medieval management of which can still be seen up the hill from Bayleaf, at the Weald and Downland Museum.

Such coppices had two tiers, the tall standard trees, and the lower coppiced underwood (that is 'copped' or beheaded). The standards were normally oak, growing some 30-100 feet apart. Long straight unknotted trunks resulted, partly from judicious pruning of the side branches 'by hook and by crook', partly by the dense underwood competition, the standards burgeoning out once they had crested the coppiced trees below. The coppiced trees were usually hazel and ash, and in wet areas, sallow. Whole blocks of these were cut to ground level every five to twenty-five years, the bases regenerating to produce a further crop of poles. The traditional bean pole is of coppiced hazel, about five years old. It is salutary to realise that an ash tree can live for two hundred years, yet periodically coppiced its bole can

Bayleaf – a re-created, late-medieval yeoman homestead, with Wealden-type house, orchard and farmyard. In the foreground is the utilitarian garden, with staked peas, and beehives on stools to prevent mice entering.

A managed hazel coppice in May. The 6- to 7-year-old rods seen here are suitable for fencing and fuel. With deep shade only the bluebells can flower, but when the coppice is felled a large variety of plants flower again.

exceed a thousand. Oak could also be pollarded, that is, felled above animal grazing height, resulting in a crop of pole-like branches.

The re-created Bayleaf shaw, researched and designed by Ruth Tittensor, is exactly the size of the original Bayleaf shaw which still exists in Kent. At 40 x 120 feet it is smaller and narrower than a full-scale coppice. The shrubs and trees here are those of the original Kent shaw, where the traditional basic standard oak and coppiced hazel and ash are augmented by species such as crab apple, field maple, holly, wild cherry, wild roses and a wild pear. The shaw is surrounded by a hawthorn hedge and when it reaches maturity it will be managed according to traditional principles, although perhaps by coppicing occasional bushes rather than the whole area in one 'fell swoop'. This will supply Bayleaf with its fencing materials, oak lath and timber poles.

YARD, ORCHARD AND GARDEN   The shaw protects the delicate plaster of one side of the Bayleaf building from the wettest winds and the farmyard and garden are enclosed on the other sides by a wattle fence and a hawthorn hedge. The latter was constructed and subsequently laid, ten years later, according to medieval principles described by Master Fitzherbert, and which still apply today (p. 63). Bob Holman, the present gardener, was surprised to know that his word 'hethering' for the long binding wands of hazel was the 'edderyng' of Fitzherbert some 450 years ago.

Within the enclosure the levelling of the cobbled stockyard, downhill from the building, created a scarp which protects the flimsy wattle and daub house walls from animal butting, such an arrangement being known in several deserted villages which have been archaeologically excavated, for instance Gomeldon. The yard is also sided by a prestigious barn and outbuildings, forming a rudimentary courtyard. In front of the house is a grassy area which would allow for turning of carts and summer meals cooked out of doors. Here both household and farm workers could sit at the trestle table, on its adjacent turf bank, under the honeysuckle arbour. There is also a forestall area with thatched hay and straw stacks, and an orchard containing the statutory minimum twelve trees, spaced thirty-six feet apart as advocated by Fitzherbert. Such spacing also allows good hay or pasture to develop, unlike the closer sixteen- to twenty-foot tree spacing of orchards in which the main function is fruit production. Crops such as vetches or beans could also be sown here, the equivalent of the unfree peasant's croft.

The well is placed conveniently near the back door, and here a tiny corner with a turf bank under a bullace tree has been fenced off with rough vertical wattle and edged outside with *gallica* roses and violets. This has the function of a small herber.

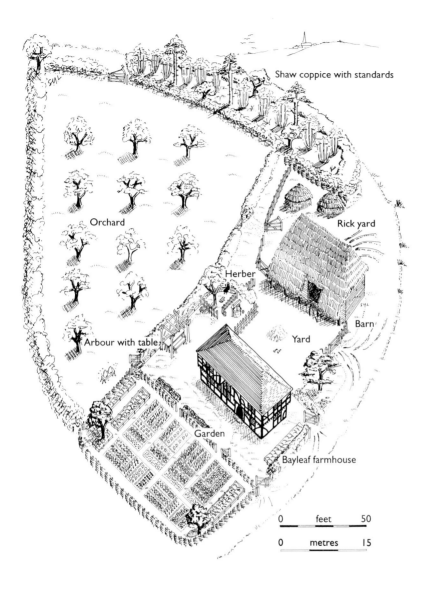

Shaw coppice with standards

Rick yard

Orchard

Herber

Barn

Yard

Arbour with table

Garden

Bayleaf farmhouse

0   feet   50

0   metres   15

Artist's impression of Bayleaf. The house and shelterbelt shaw of useful wood are typical of the Weald. Most of the garden is filled with vegetables. The leisure element is limited to a turf area in front of the house, a honeysuckle arbour giving shade over the trestle table and turf bench, and a tiny herber for small children fenced off from animals.

THE KITCHEN GARDEN The largest part of the Bayleaf garden is the vegetable and herb area, which eventually had to be enclosed by a wattle fence with concealed wire netting, to shut out the non-medieval marauding baby rabbits. The paths between the plots are of grass, which, if sickle cut, could be given as fodder to a stalled animal. The perimeter paths are economically scraped down to the flinty subsoil, the soil being worked into the beds. The path and its edge is gradually being colonised by native plants, including the apple-scented wild camomile. The vegetable garden is laid out more accurately than would have been likely in medieval times to demonstrate the underlying method, but even here we were taught a salutary lesson in design when the wattler's rectangular boundary became a trapezium due to the inherent nature of wattling!

In this kitchen garden each main plot, together with an access path, measures 2 x 1 perches (16½ x 33 feet), chosen as measurements which a medieval yeoman, particularly a bailiff, would have been accustomed to. He may even have had a perch-length stick for calculating the amount of crops on the manor. Each perch is subdivided by one-foot paths into three beds, about four feet wide and fourteen feet long, (two feet six inches being left for the path which separated it from the next perch). The plots are grouped in two lots of three, to accommodate a threefold rotation system (see illustration opposite). The size was finally decided on the basis of food for a household of six adults, the twelve perches coincidentally approximating the average ten-rod (pole or perch) twentieth-century allotment.

(see illustration opposite)

SUGGESTED THREE-YEAR CROP ROTATION CYCLE

The cycle is repeated every three years, and the plots can be of any number divisible by three. At Bayleaf there are six plots arranged in two groups of three. The plots can be of any area, but at Bayleaf each plot is two perches in area, composed of six beds.

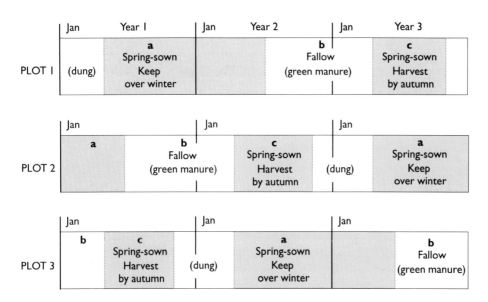

(a) *Spring-sown, keep over winter* Leeks, coleworts sown in succession from summer onwards, parsnips, leaf beet, parsley. (Garlic planted in November and over-wintered.)
(b) *Fallow* 'Edible weeds', and self-seeded crops, later turned in as green manure. Tethered animals can graze.
(c) *Spring-sown, harvest by autumn* Beans, peas, onions, spring-sown coleworts, salads, annual herbs and edible flowers.
(*Perennials in additional plot.*)

The Fromond list has been used as a guide for this garden (p. 79) and the vegetables and herbs have also been discussed on pages 28 and 77. Where necessary modern 'look-alikes' have been used, which is preferable to omitting impor-

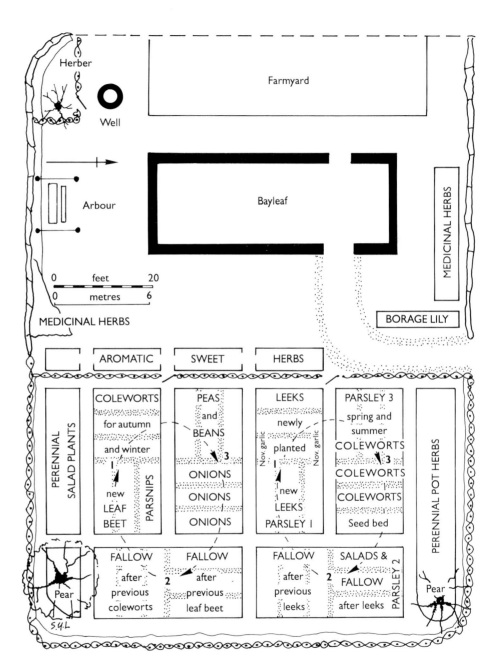

Plant-beds at Bayleaf. Three-fold rotation of crops, a miniature parallel to the crop rotation of arable fields and furlongs. Crops in the plots are 'rotated' annually. Crops in plots 1 are replaced by crops in plots 2; crops in plots 2 are replaced by crops in plots 3, etc.

tant species. An example of the positions of these crops on the ground can be seen in the illustration on the previous page, the positions changing each year, most in a clockwise direction.

The annual vegetables and herbs are grown in the perch plots, but perennial and biennial pot-herbs, which interfere with the rotation, are grown in separate areas on either side of the vegetables. Here can be found fennel, mints, alexanders, comfrey, lovage, Good King Henry, and the ever-ready green clumping onion var. *perutile*. The acid-loving native sorrel does not thrive on chalky Bayleaf soil, which demonstrates the point that one cannot be too dogmatic about 'correct' lists.

The perennial aromatic herbs which, hundreds of years earlier than the Bayleaf period (the fifteenth century), had been given pride of place in a pleasure herber, and which were still listed separately as 'sweet herbs' in catalogues as late as the eighteenth century, were a natural choice for beds opposite the house front. The soil here had to be raised twelve inches above the excavated chalk subsoil in order to add good soil, the soil being retained by wattle bed edges. Plank wood or dressed stone would have been too expensive for a bailiff. Here the handsome, lavender, hyssop, sage, savory and wild marjoram or origan have pride of place, attracting numerous bees and butterflies. Another wattle-edged bed is a living medicine basket, containing herbs, not all of which would necessarily have been planted in households of this class. Here are grown germander, betony, pennyroyal, horehound, wormwood, vervain and camomile. Only a few leaves of each would be used in tisanes. At the gate stands a stupendous clump of Madonna lilies six feet tall. Those who wish to grow such lilies should dig a hole two feet deep, beg some good chalk soil from a friend, plant the bulbs, also begged from a friend in July, just under the surface, and dust the soil annually with a little farmyard manure (or Osmocote) and ground charcoal.

BAYLEAF AS A MEDIEVAL ORGANIC GARDEN   The present-day trend towards organic gardening has its roots in Rachel Carson's innovative book *The Silent Spring*, written in 1962. It opened our eyes to the fact that even the garden shed had become filled with damaging chemicals for pest and weed control, soil fertilisation and sterilisation. Out of this has come the harking back to pre-chemical garden practices of earlier this century. Medieval dimensions can now be added to organic gardening methods as a result of the careful observations of Bob Holman, gardener at Bayleaf.

The most important difference between present-day and medieval kitchen gardening lies in the thick ground cover which becomes established in vegetable plots to retain, for the cooking pot, the many 'weeds' and self-seeding crops which today we would destroy (see asterisked entries in the Plant Index p. 142). The shortage of comments in medieval documents about pests or disease may perhaps indicate that problems were more under control than nowadays, although this does not mean that they did not exist, as we have seen from the instructions of the Goodman of Paris to his fifteen-year-old wife (p. 98). Manuscript borders, however, provide evidence for many of the insects which played an important part in the organic cycle, although aesthetic and symbolic considerations governed the choice of subjects. Ugly earthworms, slugs and larvae are never portrayed, whereas the symbolic and attractive seven-spotted ladybird, 'Our Lady's bird' representing the seven sorrows of the Virgin, sometimes appears in exaggerated form. Pollinating bees, predatory spiders, butterflies, aphid-eating lacewings and damsel flies can all be seen, as well as snails and predatory beetles. Beautiful caterpillars often grace manuscript borders, and a ceiling boss of foliage, fruit and flowers of cabbage-like density in Exeter Cathedral crawls with carved specimens.

In the Bayleaf vegetable garden the ground cover between the sown crops is composed of edible weeds, such as chickweed, fat hen, langdebeef and sowthistle, brought to a pitch of glorious technicolour by self-seeded edible garden plants such as blue borage, orange marigold and white wild camomile. Such density of growth (and the resulting green-manuring over winter) provides a miniature jungle which harbours the larval stages of many friendly insects such as hoverflies, lacewings and ladybirds, the nocturnal ground beetles which hunt slugs and snails and which also devour cabbage-root flies. The rich ground-cover keeps the upper soil moist and this not only encourages earthworms to recycle the surface decaying matter, but lessens the need for present-day, and therefore by implication, medieval, watering. It also reduces the impact of heavy rain which causes the leaching down of nutrients. When those plants which have not gone into the cooking pot have seeded, they are turned in as a green manure in early August and many seeds immediately germinate again to provide a further edible or manuring crop. A floral mixture amongst food crops and the flowers of the vegetables and herbs themselves provide nectar to feed friendly insects in their adult stages, as well as being essential in aiding the seeding process in an age when seed could not be bought. The umbelliferous flowers of parsley, skirrets, alexanders, fennel and dill attract rather nasty-looking yet friendly insects such as the ichneumon wasp. The composite flowers, such as orange marigold, white feverfew and camomile attract hoverflies in particular, who then lay their eggs next to colonies of aphids on the interplanted brassicas. In turn their larvae can consume up to 1200 aphids each. Some flowers attract aphids away from beans and cabbages, later to be eaten by insect larvae. This happens at Bayleaf with pot marigolds, but also with the English catchfly or lesser white campion which traps aphids on its sticky flower stems so successfully that Bob Holman actually transplants them to the broad bean bed, cutting them down when infected, after which they re-sprout.

At Bayleaf the surrounding wattle fence and hawthorn hedges provide a colourful wild-flower border of perennial plants such as vetches, yarrow, knapweed and hawkweeds, rich in insects and butterflies whose pesticide function has not yet been evaluated. But here, in the undisturbed shelter, ladybirds hibernate. They are of key importance, their adults being attracted by nectar and aphid honeydew, and their larvae having a voracious appetite for aphids. Ichneumon wasps lay their eggs in cabbage white caterpillars and consume them, the empty caterpillar skins being visible to an observant gardener.

The story is still unfolding and we only have a glimmering of the delicate balance in this miniature world of webs and cycles. We have not yet spoken of the part played by birds and other butterflies. Early in the morning bluetits, for instance, can be seen eating the cabbage white larvae. But what is the effect, direct or indirect, of all the other birds observed in and around and above Bayleaf: wren, robin, corn bunting, tree pippit, meadow pippit, yellow hammer and overhead the skylark, little owl and sparrowhawk? What parts are played by the numerous butterflies: the small, common and holly blues, the green veined white, the small brown, and the orange tip; the small tortoise shell, red admiral and peacock, meadow brown, small skipper and gatekeeper?

We have, therefore, at Bayleaf a mixed vegetable and herb garden on chalky soil, in full sunlight, worked with the benefit of well rotted cow and pig manure, whose plant composition has taken four years to develop. Provided the vegetables, even onions, are kept weed-free for their first month, and totally free of the true weeds, such as dock, common thistle and nettle, they do not suffer from later competition from 'edible' weeds. Weeds which become too exuberant can always be reduced. Those of us who are bored with conventional vegetable gardening may be tempted to follow the same methods, using clippings from leeks for soup rather than expecting a large white base, or cooking some green-stage onions entire rather than leaving the bulbs for uncertain maturity. However, it should be remembered that the Bayleaf farmstead is isolated, pristine and surrounded by several hundred acres of Sussex countryside. Our urban gardens are enclosed by fences, not hedgerows, our neighbours safeguard themselves with masks whilst blanket-spraying and weed-killing, destroying friend and foe alike. There are no perfect insects left to fly into our garden, and we ourselves reduce our own natural habitats by tidying up every grass tussock or decaying piece of wood, turning every stone, hoeing dry soil to a sterilised state. Such gardens as Bayleaf are not made in a day and it is naïve to

Bayleaf. The hazel wattle fence has a gate of oak-lath trellis. A hazel wattle-edged bed contains hyssop. Beyond lies the vegetable garden with seeding leek heads.

Bayleaf, showing how the edible weed plot becomes a mass of colour in July. Self-sown yellow and orange pot marigold, wild camomile and corn poppy can be seen.

A turf seat from a text written for the common man. A simple woman, rather than the Virgin, is sitting on a turf seat spinning, singing a lullaby and rocking the cradle simultaneously. Adam is using a one-footed spade with its iron 'shoe'. 15th century.

think that an undisturbed natural balance is always in favour of man, yet why such additional beauty of sound and colour?

THE MISTRESS OF THE HOUSE   The building derived its name from several generations of Baileys who occupied it. Mistress Bailey would have tended the garden herself, to provide food for her husband, two or three children, servants and perhaps retired parents. The garden would supply ingredients for her vegetable pottage (including the self-seeded 'weeds'), salads and a few green sauces cooked on the central hearth. After anchoring her washing on the hawthorn hedge she could justify a rest on the turf seat of the herber, provided she spun, sang a lullaby and rocked the cradle with her foot simultaneously.

She would also have a rudimentary knowledge of medicine. Bayleaf in its original position was the only homestead on a road connecting two valleys, and many a courier on horseback would have stopped overnight and slept beside the fire 'hard side down, cold side up'. Perhaps a pedlar with a chesty cough might be given a hot infusion of hyssop or horehound: a bruised knee might be treated with a green poultice of hot boiled cabbage or leek, overlaid with sheeps' wool. Largesse was not only the prerogative of the lady of the manor.

Periodic sweepings from the floors would have been put out into the central rubbish heap in the yard, together with bones, feathers, etc, which would be later returned to the garden or to fields. Fennel, mints and vermicidal wormwood and mugwort would then be strewn on the floor, and flowers brought in to deck up the house in 'pots, pails and tubs'. Finally Tusser's thumb-nail sketch of the housewife's evening ends the day:

> Make servant at night lug in wood or a log
> Let none come in empty but slut and thy dog
> No clothes in the garden no trinkets without
> No doore leave unbolted for fear of a dout [thief].
> Wash dishes, lay leavens, save fire and away,
> Lock doores and to bed a good housewife will say.
> Thou woman whom pitie becometh the best
> Graunt all that hath laboured time to take rest.

Hangleton: A Retired Peasant's Garden of the Thirteenth Century

The village of Hangleton in Sussex was deserted by the sixteenth century, and its building foundations were investigated before they were finally gouged out of the earth for a railway cutting (Holden, 1963; Hurst, 1964). A one-room building of the thirteenth century with an oven, and which had probably been a second building within a close, perhaps a bakehouse, was reconstructed at the Weald and Downland Museum and is now named 'Hangleton', after the village. The museum brief was to design a suitable garden for it, which is now in the process of construction.

The only way to justify a re-created garden was to think of it as an area set aside for a retired peasant, within a larger holding. Retirement contracts were drawn up between unfree peasants and their successors when old age, at around fifty, had reduced their agricultural abilities. Many retirement contracts allowed a place beside the fire, a bed and certain garden crops, or use of part of a garden or even half the produce of a fruit tree, a beehive or a place to fatten up a weaned piglet. The following is a more generous example drawn up between Elyas and his son John in 1298:

And the aforesaid Elyas until Michaelmas next will have all said land properly tilled and sown at his own cost, of which land he and Christina his wife will fully receive half of the whole crop. And for the rest, the aforesaid John will find for the same Elyas and Christina his wife honorable sustenance in food and drink so long as they live, and they will dwell with the aforesaid John in lodging on the chief messuage. And if it chance (which God forbid) that quarrels and discords arise in time to come between the parties, so that they cannot dwell together peaceably in one house, the aforesaid John will find for the same Elyas and Christina, or for whichever one survives the other, a house in his courtyard, with curtilage, where they can honorably dwell.

Hangleton – a re-created retired peasant couple's garden, c.1300. An area within the garden is enclosed by a 'dead hedge' and contains beds of 'cut and come again' plants – parsley, leeks cut like chives, coleworts, bulb and green onions. A few plants are left to seed. A piglet would have been fattened each year and killed in November for bacon.

The Hangleton re-creation represents just such a curtilage, or private fenced-off area. Our fragmentary knowledge of peasant gardens has already been put to good use at Bayleaf, which represents the highest level of free peasant or yeoman holding. At the most minimal level imaginable a painting by Brueghel shows a peasant couple's garden of about seven by seven feet, wattle fenced and containing seven colewort or kale plants, these being economically harvested leaf by leaf (see p. 118). 'Weeds', invisible beneath the snow-covered garden would have been added to the pottage. The Hangleton plot has been re-created at a level between these two extremes, similar to the tiny gardens portrayed in a drawing of Paignton (see p. 45)

Within the fenced area of the reconstruction, as illustrated above, there is a border for perennial plants such as ever-ready green onions, hyssop and sage, and some second-year parsley for seed. A path is lined with the huge six- to eight-inch

Detail from The Numbering at Bethlehem *by Pieter Brueghel the Younger,* showing an elderly couple's garden. This could equally represent a subsidiary house and garden within a larger close, of some two hundred years earlier. The seven colewort plants would be picked on a 'cut and come again principle'. 16th century.

local flints, even as the nearby allotments are today. These allow the soil level to be raised above the inhospitable sub-soil of the plot, the infertile nature of the ground adjacent to frequent rebuilding having been noted in the villages such as Wharram Percy. January scourings from ditches, house sweepings, and bracken litter from the pigsty could all have been used to build up a soil. For economy of edging, one larger area, as constructed here, fourteen by eight feet, is tramped across to make three beds, planted in rudimentary rotation. One is for leeks, leaf beet and parsley, one for spring and summer coleworts, the third for the second year sprouting of leaf beet and parsley till July, followed by coleworts for winter, all with an undercrop of edible weeds. The leeks would not be transplanted but cut as soup leeks like chives. Here is a medieval 'cut and come again' garden; one does not kill the goose that lays the golden egg.

A part of the existing scarp bank has been levelled off as a turf-topped seat, overhung with the honeysuckle and sweetbriar which was already growing there, giving a place to sit in the sun and perhaps make a bee-skep using the age-old tools of chicken-bone channel and curved cow-horn funnel which nestles in the hand. Did our peasant Elyas ever sit in such a corner, content with the order of things, with ox horn for hand, hive for the bee, wax for the altar candle, honey for man?

Sir Roger Vaughan's Garden at Tretower Court: A Fifteenth-Century Courtier's Garden

Tretower Court nestles in the peaceful Usk Valley, near Crickhowell in Wales. Overhead the sky is filled with darting, diving swallows which return each year to the old grey roofs, as their forebears may have done since medieval times. The well-defended group of buildings was transformed by the Yorkist Sir Roger Vaughan, a supporter of Edward IV. Here a fifteenth-century garden to suit the life and time of such a courtier was re-created by Elisabeth Whittle in 1991 and has been subse-

Sir Roger Vaughan's Garden at Tretower Court, Powys, showing diagonal-patterned fencing, checkerboard layout, and raised beds used as seats. A flowering mead lies behind.

quently nurtured by Frances Kay. The convincingly re-created features and authentic planting are a vision of what could well have been found here 500 years ago, even though no garden remains have survived for restoration. This garden is important since similar features could have enhanced odd corners of the nearby sumptuous palace of Raglan Castle which was vastly extended by Sir Roger's half-brother. There, according to an early fifteenth-century document, extensive orchards were 'full of apple trees and plums and figs and cherries and grapes, and French plums, and pears, and nuts, and every fruit that is sweet and delicious' (Whittle, 1989).

The Tretower garden re-creation is sheltered by perimeter planting of early varieties of apple trees with tree seats, and by a magnificent flat-topped oak pergola of 'carpenter's work', some forty yards in length, clothed with the white climbing *Rosa alba*, vines and native honeysuckle, and under-planted with a succession of herbaceous plants such as cream-flowered lily of the valley, Solomon's seal and woodruff, pink and white campion, blue cornflower and columbine. Many of these self-seed.

Elsewhere diagonal-patterned split-rod trellises are now weathered to a silver colour, blending with the grey sandstone building. They enclose a turf-seated herber where the red and white roses, *Rosa gallica* and *Rosa alba*, are underplanted with camomile, betony and strawberry. Beside the herber lies a checkerboard arrangement of five-foot alternating squares of turf and herbaceous beds, the latter containing many of the ornamental plants listed elsewhere, such as peony, iris and Madonna lily. The central bed now has a fountain in the form of a pedestalled bowl, from which the water soothingly drips into the surrounding pool.

The remainder of the garden is filled with a flowering mead, cleverly interpreted from medieval illustrations. Several rectangles of turf, cut in May and again in September, are set amongst grass paths which are mown monthly. Within the bed areas pernicious weeds such as dock are spot weed-killed, thus also suppressing the surrounding grass. This gives spaces in which to plant choice wild flowers. The spring celandines, primroses and cowslips are followed by mowing, and then after a pause by the later and taller knapweed, hawkweeds, field geranium, vetches, ox-eye daisies, toadflax and campions, which are gradually being planted.

As in all medieval gardens the observer should learn to enjoy the present moment to the full, the fleeting period of a single flower in its prime, the immediacy of aromatic herbs bruised in the hand. For its overwhelming moment of glory Tretower Court garden should not be missed in late June or early July for its display of *Rosa alba*, intermingled with pink foxgloves on the forty-yard pergola. Neither a painting, nor the written word, nor a photograph can be a substitute for the experience of air which is redolent with the scent of one thousand white roses.

> O Rose, this painted rose
> Is not the whole.
> Who paints the flower
> Paints not its fragrant soul.
>
> (*Carmina Burana*, 13th century)

Queen Eleanor's Garden: A Royal Thirteenth-Century Herber

The castle at Winchester was in its domestic heyday in the second part of the thirteenth century and was a fit home for two sophisticated continental queens. It was embellished with gardens, under the instruction of Henry III who in 1235 built the Great Hall and ordered the making of 'three herbers in this castle'. The inspiration for the re-creation of a royal garden covering the period from the construction of the Hall until the castle was gutted by fire in 1302 came from the Hampshire Gardens Trust, and the vision became reality in 1986 in the hands of the Architect's Department of Hampshire County Council. The garden is named after Eleanor of Provence and her daughter-in-law Eleanor of Castile, the French and

Castilian queens of Henry III and his son Edward I. Eleanor of Aquitaine only sojourned in the castle as a prisoner in its earlier defensive days. The exact sizes and positions of the three herbers are unknown since they lay between buildings which no longer exist, namely the complex of newly built king's and queen's chambers and six chapels, but a turf area certainly lay on the south side of the Great Hall, near the kitchens. We also know that one garden was repaired some thirty years after it was made. There were additional turf areas, an enclosed falcon mews just outside the west gate of the castle and at least one dovecot.

The chosen plot for the garden re-creation was a totally enclosed triangle of ground, some ten by thirty yards nestling on the sunny side of the Great Hall, and never built on for 700 years. However, the Victorian red brick barracks rose up from an eight-foot podium not five yards ahead. This podium was the base of the seventeenth-century King's Palace built by Christopher Wren, the first 'vandal' who submerged many medieval castle buildings here. To the east, where once a handsome curtain wall had stood, the yellow brick back of the newly constructed Law Courts towered fifty feet, its lower level punctuated by seven louvred ventilators, each twelve feet high. On the ground there flourished dock, nettle and convolvulus. Below ground there was worse to come for here there lay the foundations of earlier buildings, infilled with rubble and even concrete, and horsetail rhizomes penetrated to a depth of eight feet. An enormous challenge lay ahead.

DESIGNING THE GARDEN   The medieval use of such a garden had to be borne in mind. This was not to be a physic or kitchen garden but one in which a queen such as Eleanor of Castile might sit and play chess, perhaps using the jasper and crystal chess set given to her by Edward I. There would have to be sitting space for her six or seven damsels-in-waiting too, perhaps a shady arbour to walk in, and herbs to pick and bruise in the hand, while servants beneath a pentice carried dishes from the nearby kitchens to the great dining hall (see illustration p. 123).

Should the garden be filled with medieval colour by incorporating patterned tiled paving and brilliant flowers, highlighted by gilding and heraldic objects – a 'merrie' garden? Or was it to reflect the purity of chivalry by following Henry III's penchant for whitewashed buildings and white-blossomed trees of cherry and pear, with even the walls behind turf seats carefully whitewashed as he had arranged at Clarendon Palace, near Salisbury? Alas, neither was possible, the former because of expense, the latter because one cannot whitewash Law Courts, or listed Wren structures, be they even so humble as a podium wall. It was finally decided that an overall spirit of the past could be evoked with the chivalric quality of fidelity as a central theme, as symbolised by the permanence of evergreen plants such as turf, holly, bay and ivy, with scented foliage being as important as flowers. In this way the garden would not have to rely for its impact on the fleeting flowers of the unreliable plants of the period, but rather these colourful ephemera would punctuate the evergreen plants in brilliant bursts – iris and peony in May, roses in June and lilies in July. Thus the twentieth-century appetite for flower, form and colour, rather than foliage and scent, would be satisfied. As with all gardens moments of inner and outer peace have to be treasured, and in a quiet oasis in a busy city, whether of the thirteenth or the twentieth century, even a single flower is a sufficient aid for meditation.

THE CONSTRUCTION Once there is an overall designer's impression it is possible to concentrate on the individual jigsaw pieces, choosing from the wide range of features those which could be tailored to fit the tiny plot. The making of the garden was in itself a process of discovery, revealing the degree of authenticity that was achievable in the twentieth century, with a dialogue being established between the designer and each craftsman. It is the craftsman who is the living bearer of an oral and manual tradition, largely undocumented throughout the centuries. Where possible nearby examples of the craft were observed so that craftsmen could copy them and the purist be satisfied.

A team was assembled in addition to the designers and the job architect, which comprised a master stonemason, a carver and a wheelwright, together with carpenters, a blacksmith, a roof shingler, a plumber and a bronze-caster. There were also the workmen who carted and levelled and laid hard-core, gravel and paving, and gardeners who propagated and planted, laid turf and made turf seats. Much work was done with mechanical excavators and power barrows which had to reach the site by clever weaving between the priceless Purbeck marble columns of the Hall.

In laying out gardens the advice of Albertus Magnus, writing in 1260, is still followed to this day: first levelling, then weed-killing, albeit done more successfully using chemicals rather than the boiling water advocated by Albertus. Purbeck limestone was the obvious choice for the stonework, matching the same stone used in the Hall, not too soft but with a porosity allowing a mellowing colonisation of each minute surface pit by algae. As the mason pointed out, the surface would thereby reach perfection with age. This stone was hand-chiselled and was also used for kerb edging, walling, stone benches, channel pool, fountain (see illustration p. 127) and paving. The benches were copied from the window seats in the Hall, and the fountain column was copied from the 1292 tomb of Peter de Sancto Mario which can be seen in the nearby thirteenth-century hospice of St Cross. The

Queen Eleanor's Garden, Winchester. This artist's impression of the re-created 13th-century royal castle garden shows the Great Hall, fountain and channel, tunnel vine arbour, trellised 'Queen's herber' with turf-topped benches, stone benches and herbaceous borders.

fountain was based on the description already given (p. 60) and a full-size drawing of the column was held up in the garden for size and used by the mason as the basis of his work, as had always been done with cathedral carvings, drawn lifesize on parchment or scratched on a plaster floor. It was decided that the falcon which tops the fountain would face the door exit, with eyes at a height to stare one in the face since the relationship of falconer to falcon was that of knight to lady, and he was not worthy who could not look his falcon in the eye. A basis for the falcon design for the top of the fountain was eventually found after a long hunt, carved *c.*1308 in the beautiful choirstalls of Winchester Cathedral itself. Here the falcon sits with wings crossed as in numerous illustrations, on the gauntlet-covered hand of a kind-faced falconer whose eyes are shielded against the sun by a peaked cap.

A water channel was known in the Queen's Garden at Wolvesley Palace on the other side of Winchester, where Edward I's new queen resided in 1306. This idea was also copied, the natural slope of the garden giving a flow that was neither too sluggish nor too hurried. Its rippling surface brings to mind a medieval Hispano-Arab poem in which such a channel is compared to a writhing snake, and is of relevance to the background of Eleanor of Castile. For the tunnel arbour (see back cover ilustration) a wheelwright gypsy caravan-maker was found. The thirty-five foot tunnel was finally built from curved conifer poles, set eighteen inches apart and attached to each other by horizontal poles. The poles were tied at the top to a minimal metal framework, which was felt to be necessary in case children tried to use it as a climbing frame. The stranded fencing wire ties, imitating medieval withies, are almost invisible. The trellises were to be constructed with four foot-high oak frames of 3 x 3 inch timber, and square-crossed coniferous wood poles.

The twelve-foot ventilator shafts in the Law Courts wall were concealed behind a magnificent pentice designed by the architect, just as a pentice had linked the kitchens and hall of Henry III's nearby Clarendon Palace. The Winchester pentice is roofed with oak shingles, as the Great Hall itself had once been, and the rafter ends and the steep roof pitch which was typical of medieval buildings were copied from the restored thirteenth-century fine merchant's house in French Street, Southampton. The roof has now already acquired the appearance of an old bird's ruffled feathers, and it houses the white doves.

A small herber fit for a queen was constructed, not much more than an exedra inspired by a manuscript illumination (illustrated on the front cover), but the turf seats are now faced with stone for easier maintenance, and the archway was personalised by using the heraldic device of Eleanor of Castile's family, purple lion on white, gold castle on red, the same decoration being incorporated on the pillow of the exquisite gilded tomb in which she still lies embalmed in Westminster Abbey.

THE PLANTS   We have a clear picture of the plants which were grown in the thirteenth century from the researches of John Harvey, and additional knowledge of their growth habits together with evidence from medieval illustration has helped us to understand how they were grown. It may seem surprising that it is easier to find authentic plants for a medieval ornamental garden than for a seventeenth-century one, the reason being that the majority were originally grown in their native European form, and are therefore still available. The additional ornamental plants which were already of great antiquity in the thirteenth century are still available as 'cottage garden' plants, namely the red and white rose, Madonna lily, flag irises, peonies and granny's bonnet columbines. In only a few cases have we been tempted to use modern cultivars on account of their bushier and more durable form, such as the wallflower 'Gold Bedder', and the wild heartsease 'Johnny Jump-Up' since even in these the flower is still virtually the same.

The centre of the garden is filled with turf, because an expanse of green in a garden serves the same purpose as space in art, silence in music or a pause in speech. Its psychological value was well understood in medieval times in the provision of a green cloister garth, just as it is still necessary today in any garden. The aim in Queen Eleanor's garden is to achieve a short neat turf, kept evergreen even in drought by night-time irrigation. To avoid too modern an appearance the mowing is done with a rotary mower, and the turf is punctuated with an even flush of daisies from March to July, representing the purest form of flowering mead. Roses and honeysuckle are the first choice to ornament the perimeter trellises, particularly the low bushy red *Rosa gallica*, emblem of Eleanor of Provence, and the tall and robust white *Rosa alba*, which were later named the roses of Lancaster and York. These two ancient garden roses also clothe the sides of the tunnel arbour, the white rose having the advantage of doing well in a north-facing position. The damask rose, which is the most ill-formed and ill-coloured but most superbly scented of all roses, had not reached England by the medieval period.

For shade, the top of the thirty-five-foot tunnel is arched by vines grown between the same roses, vines having similar requirements. Every vine has a vertical leader and its winter-pruned spurs which are set at one-foot intervals produce leafy shoots in May, each shoot bearing bunches of grapes by late summer. No vine varieties have been named for the period, but two vines which do well in England are the white 'Madeline Angevine' and the black 'Leon Millot', the leaves of both giving a delightful translucent shade. A vine of everlasting life was sometimes symbolically grown over a church or building entrance, and the doorway of the Hall has therefore been adorned with the black-graped 'Wrotham Pinot'. Additional garden shade is given by the fig tree and the Glastonbury thorn whose origin goes back in the mists of time to the occasion when it reputedly grew from Joseph of Aramathea's staff as he forced it into the ground to mark the founding of the monastery at Glastonbury.

Hawthorn, sweetbriar and honeysuckle make a classic deciduous hedge, completing the enclosure of the garden, and even common ivy forms an attractive evergreen screen, grown on a firm trellis. It has a surprisingly resinous scent in the sun after a shower of cleansing rain, and the screen can be kept in shape by cutting evenly spaced shoots back to their base in spring with an additional all-over clipping every five or six years. Further large specimen plants give structure and are usefully evergreen, namely holly, bay, savin, and also the gold-flowering broom which was once named *Planta genista* – the badge flower of the Plantagenets including Henry III and Edward I. We have little guidance about the arrangement of plants in medieval borders, since artists who were restricted by the stiff art of the wood-cut naturally have to show plants more sparsely spaced than they would have been, and others working with paint or embroidery covered every inch of soil. A clue is given in a damp-stained vellum letter in the British Library written from a prison cell by a sixteenth-century aristocrat, Sir Thomas Tresham, to his steward, which states: 'and beneath the roses red and white, plant periwinkle and wild strawberries, to serve the weeding'. These two plants, together with the brilliant blue germander speedwell and the invasive ground ivy can fight out a battle beneath taller perennials, forming a complete mat in the process. However, they do not always do battle with an eye to aesthetics and in a public garden we have found it safer to limit them, using periwinkle as an edging plant, as if about to invade, in front of taller perennials. Within this two-tier system the tallest perennials are grown at the back of the borders.

ABOVE *The Queen's herber at Queen Eleanor's Garden, Winchester.* This rose-trellised exedra is based on the front cover illustration. It is entered by the arch to the right. The roses are *Rosa alba* and *R. gallica.* The turf seats have now been fronted with stone.

For the choice of border plants, once again Albertus Magnus gives us a basic principle to follow, namely plants 'to delight the sight and the smell'. He then suggests rue, sage, basil, violet, columbine, lily, rose, iris 'and the like', to which fennel, winter savory, wormwood and hyssop can justifiably be added as aromatic herbs. His flowers all have a deep Christian significance, but for the Winchester garden we can also justify other native Mediterranean plants such as the pot marigold, the Spanish rose or hollyhock, and perhaps lavender and wallflower, since they are quite likely to have been introduced by Queen Eleanor of Castile.

Part of the art of gardening is to keep up a changing interest throughout the year, and perhaps we can imagine that the Aragonese gardeners of Eleanor of Castile might have been sent into the Hampshire countryside to find north-European native flowers new to her, for her delight. There would be periwinkle and primroses in March, bluebells in April, Solomon's seal and lily of the valley, cowslips and broom for May, to be grown side by side with common European garden plants such as red peonies, *Peonia mascula*, and *Peonia officinalis*, the purple flag iris, and the white counterpart *Iris florentina*, all of them fleeting. Other native plants which periodically grace dry or shady corners are the gladdon iris, *Iris foetidissima*, the greater celandine, and ferns such as hartstongue, polypody and the feathered lady-fern *Athyrium filix-femina*. June is the month of the red and white

RIGHT *The gothic-style fountain at Queen Eleanor's Garden,* with four leopard-head masks and surmounting bronze falcon, is based on a description from Charing Cross Mews, *c.*1275. The water channel, daisy turf, stone seat and Glastonbury hawthorn tree are also shown.

roses, which together with honeysuckle scent the air headily in early morning and late evening. Madonna lilies grace the month of July with overwhelming scent and beauty but we have found that no plant dies an uglier-looking or worse-smelling death. Perhaps this is one reason why they were usually illustrated in removable pots, the image of untainted perfection being maintained. From late July to August the flowering herbs play their part, with a white spangling of camomile, mauve 'Old English' lavender, rich blue hyssop and pale yellow-flowered fennel.

This stream of beauty would seem to be sufficient, but in practice we are left for half the year with plants going to seed from July onwards and no further flowers until a few shy violets appear in March. In addition, each of these plants bears flowers for only two or three weeks in the year, after which it occupies the ground as an unspectacular specimen for some fifty additional weeks. This limitation is counteracted in later medieval gardens by the introduction of the valuable long-flowering and scented pinks and carnations, but these were not known in thirteenth-century gardens. Many early forms of aromatic herbs such as savory, marjoram, sage, and thyme look grey and uninteresting with tiny mauve flowers, and are not even particularly air-scenting. Such limitations would not be important if we experienced a garden as the medieval man or woman did, extending the impact of plants beyond their flowering period by picking little handfuls of aromatic leaves to crush and release the scent, to stroke for their softness, even to chew tiny buds for savour. We have tried to compensate with extra floral interest by threading a time-ribbon, so to speak, of annuals and biennials, grown as 'bedding'. That is, we increase the flower power by filling gaps and using some border space twice over, in the bedding out of young nursery-grown plants, between the larger perennials and herbs. This is in fact merely a tidying up of a natural cottage garden process.

The planting schemes at Winchester are gradually being perfected, under the relentless pressure of public interest every day of the year. Through re-creation of gardens we have learnt about the short flowering period of medieval plants and the fact that our present way of experiencing gardens is different, being largely dominated by the eye. We are reminded of the peripatetic nature of the medieval court, where perhaps each garden would have had a particular season of delight. There were, of course, three herbers at Winchester Castle, and perhaps one was visited for only a few peak weeks when it was filled solidly in late June and early July with scented roses on the trellises, Madonna lilies in pots everywhere and huge second-year clumps of perfumed and foaming sweet rocket filling all the borders.

Rhuddlan Castle: An Imagined Royal Thirteenth-Century Herber

One of the pleasures for a garden historian is being an arm-chair detective squeezing every scrap of detail out of the given documents. There are tantalising details of materials used to construct a garden in 1282 in the newly built Rhuddlan Castle in Wales, where Queen Eleanor was having a building made for her goldsmith, with plans for a tiny garden in the central courtyard. Minimal details of materials and instructions are given in her accounts (Colvin, 1963). Could we reconstruct a garden from these? Six thousand turves, perhaps of fine sea-washed quality from the tidal river, were brought down by boat to turf the 80 x 90 foot trapezoidal courtyard which still exists. Encircling the well, which had a boarded roof (perhaps as the one illustrated here) and was situated in one quadrant of the courtyard, a 'little fishpond' was to be made, lined with the four cart-loads of clay brought from the nearby marshes. Seats were to be set around it made by Willelmo le Plomer, and tun barrels were to be used for fencing (as could be seen in Cornwall up to the Second World War). No stone is mentioned for the seats or the pool edging, and it is therefore probable that it was not used, turf or timber being more likely, since stone was expensive and would have been entered in the accounts. If timber revetting was used for the pool sides a square rather than a circular pool would be the most likely.

A fount or well with timber canopy, in an illustration from Chaucer's translation of the *Roman de la Rose*.

Six thousand machine-cut turves of present-day size would have turfed 18,000 square feet, vastly more than the 7250 square feet of the trapezoidal courtyard which still exists today. We do not know the size of a medieval turf, but quantities of material have always related to man's ability to lift them, so a more crudely cut medieval turf, twice as thick, but the same weight, would have been half the size of a modern piece of turf, that is 1 x 1½ feet. A square shape even smaller would not have allowed for the staggering of joins. Even on this basis there would have been some twelve hundred turves left over. Could these turves have been used for turf seats? Stacked ten layers high and giving a bench width of eighteen inches there would have been enough turves left to make a bench of one hundred and twenty feet in length, or formed as a perimeter square with thirty-foot sides.

We cannot estimate the size of the pool from the cartloads of clay, but a square well of four to six feet, and a 'little pool' of five to six feet around it might occupy a central square of, say, fourteen feet. Thus there would be a turf space of some six to seven feet all round, between the pool edge and the seat, narrow enough to watch the fish whilst sitting, but wide enough to net them out.

The fencing was made from tun barrels. According to a cooper a tun barrel was fifty inches high, with a belly of forty-five inches diameter, and almost straight-sided. Its slightly tapered staves were five to six inches wide and about two inches thick. When released from its hoops and dried out the slight curve would become straight. Each barrel would give about twelve feet of close-board fencing, allowing for wastage and perhaps pointing of the tops if the staves were used vertically. Thus about ten barrels would be required. If there was a need for privacy the barrel palings, if fifty inches long and used vertically, would have to be lifted about sixteen inches at least from the ground, above eye height. We can imagine Willelmo the Plomer, who was employed to make the seats, perhaps constructing a carpenter's framework to raise the staves to 5½–6 feet, forming both the seat backs and the garden fence simultaneously. A gate could also be constructed. Since fish need flowing water the well-head was probably of the spring type, with a channel flowing from it, and a plank bridge would also be needed for access to the well. Whilst a mathematician would doubt the validity of solving a problem with so many unknowns, and the ignoring of some details, these deductions lead to a challenging idea for a minimal garden. Our medieval gardener would, of course, have had a simpler job, by first knowing the size of the pool and turf seating before deciding the amount of turf to order!

We have described a central spring-type well feeding a surrounding square fish-pond, and some six to seven feet away a border of turf seats backed by a six-foot high fence made from barrel staves, the whole garden being about thirty feet square. Perhaps we can imagine our past Castilian queen sitting in the sun in such turf-benched privacy at least some of the day, enjoying the movements of the bream or pike from her seat, and displaying to her guests the jewellery which her resident goldsmith has just completed in his workshop newly constructed at the castle.

These arguments represent the first steps which a researcher might take with evidence from an original document in order to re-create an authentic garden. Further support might then be sought from illustrations, such as on p. 1. There could perhaps be a second gate for the use of those collecting water from the well, or a subsidiary pool outside the fencing into which the channel water could flow. A tree could be planted outside the enclosed area on the south side to provide shade. Plants could be added, such as scented herbs on the seat tops, and the turf seats could be widened, leaving a space between the turf and the fencing in order to grow roses or vines, perhaps adding a willow-rod arbour instead of a tree. The garden could also be enlarged. A convincing garden could thus materialise, its design guided by consideration of the principles of authenticity, practicality and aesthetics.

A Garden of Love. The features of this herber could be re-created in a corner of a present-day garden of any size. Brick and turf-topped seats can also be used to lean against when sitting on floor cushions on the lawn. Roses grow on the trellis, a jet of water flows into a pool, a table is covered with a cloth. A convenient lawn lies beyond. Italian, 15th century.

6
Make Your Own Medieval Garden

Those who wish to have a small totally medieval-style garden can adapt ideas from the many contemporary illustrations (in particular the classic small garden illustrated on p. 16), using the plant list given on p. 79, but I myself would not do this, because of the fleeting and periodic beauty of such gardens. However there are several individual features which can embellish a present-day garden to advantage.

Expense will play a large part in how you choose to construct any of the features described below. However in your own home you are not subject to the rigorous standards necessary for a public re-creation, and following the spirit rather than the letter of medieval gardening, you can use several products from garden centres and builders' merchants to good effect, such as ready-constructed softwood trellis panels instead of split-oak lath, or concrete blocks camouflaged to look like whitewashed, medieval stone ashlar. Standard instructions for postholes and foundations can be obtained from a practical book such as *The Garden-Making Manual* (1985) by P. McHoy.

A Trellised Herber

The range of size and detail encompassed in a herber has already been described. Here we are using it in its smallest sense as a trellised place, whether free-standing or in the L-shape of a corner wall, or partitioned off at the end of your garden, where it can add an air of intrigue, particularly if it has a lockable gate.

When choosing a site for your herber bear in mind whether you want shade or sun. The answer is likely to be both, in which case place it near to a neighbouring tree whose shade changes with the position of the sun. There need be no limit to how large your herber is, but the tiny herber in Queen Eleanor's garden which is based on the Boccaccio painting of Emilia, is the smallest that can be built. There, due to lack of space, the surrounding trellis is mounted into the perimeter turf bench, and the central flowery lawn is only 6 x 8 feet. For a larger herber an authentic model to adapt to your liking can be seen in a roundel engraved by a fifteenth-century artist (opposite), and the most basic arrangement is illustrated on p. 134.

The essential element in any herber is the seat. This can be in the form of a timber or brick-walled 'box', filled with rubble and soil and turfed with thyme, marjoram or grass, or an L-shaped or exedra bench as described below. It should be placed against the trellis perimeter so that the lawn can be easily maintained.

There is often a problem in cutting turf in such small areas, even if mowed without a box. The neatest, although most sterile, solution is to use pea-gravel, but this requires a 3-4 inch board against the soil borders. I would probably choose periwinkle, *Vinca minor*, planted at 6-8 inch intervals, mixed with wild strawberry if you wish. Once established it can occasionally be sheared and the ground can be spiked with a fork in autumn to decrease compaction. A camomile (*Anthemis nobilis*) lawn is advisable only if you are prepared for a brown mess from October to April, followed by replanting in May with tufts of seedlings at 4-6 inch intervals which have been grown as a turf in seed trays. Then you must shear it at four-week intervals till the end of June, watering copiously in drought, and thereafter leave it to flower. There is no type of planting more beautiful than a camomile lawn in full flower in the sun, with its scent wafting in the air as you lie on it, but do not expect to have it all year round, or without labour.

If you wish to have scent in the herber it is best to allow a two feet six inch to three feet border. In it can be grown a few climbing roses, honeysuckle and vines, trained along the trellis and pruned using the same method as the vine arbour (below). You may not want to limit yourself to the authentic *Rosa alba* or *gallica* which flower for only two to three weeks, but do at least plant scented roses. The other plants to be included as a start are fennel and winter savory which combine to give a mouth-watering peppery scent. Hyssop, lavender, sage and rosemary are essential, for bruising in the hand.

The size of your herber will depend finally on the available space, what features you wish to include, and the amount of trellis you can afford. Take some chairs to your chosen area and line them up to estimate the minimum sitting space. Mark out the 'carpet' area and the borders with bamboo sticks, or string, and see what looks the right size for your particular needs. This will give an idea of the amount of trellis needed, and the entrance position. Garden centre trellis panels can be used unless you are determined to achieve strict authenticity. Diagonal-patterned trellis is preferable to a square pattern since it is closer to the original medieval diagonal split lath. The square trellis panels are produced in framed standard sizes of 6 feet by 1–6 feet, but the diagonal trellis of the same size is only available unframed. Both need to be incorporated onto or into a standard four inch by three inch timber framework. Aim for a fence of a maximum height of five feet six inches or a minimum of four feet which will give a feeling of enclosure when you are seated. If possible have a gate, or at least an arch, as a doorway to your 'pretty parlour'.

There is no doubt that the effect of genuine split-oak trellises and oak framework, with their silver colour on ageing, justifies the extra labour, and it is worth hunting for lath from local woodland firms. If pliable enough the lath should be interwoven, which increases its rigidity, aiming for diamonds of about six inches wide and eight inches high (measured from the lath centres). If not interwoven then copper nails or rivets are necessary at every crossing. Both machine-made and split-oak lattice panels should be kept in place on the framework by beading. Any preservative will spoil the silver ageing process.

BENCH Benches can be placed against a wall or in an L-shaped corner, and they can also be free-standing. Brick or stone bases are preferable to timber bases. The measurements depend upon how you intend to use them, but a minimum functional size is a height of fifteen to seventeen inches, a width of eighteen inches and length of about five feet, enabling two conversing people to turn towards each other. Such a bench can be made as a hollow wall of five tiers of bricks, the cavity being filled with rubble and soil. Turf is difficult to maintain on the top, and the gold-tipped compact form of wild marjoram, *Origanum vulgare compactum*, sometimes named golden marjoram or *O. aureum*, is the best choice. It can be tidied up in spring and will remain neat all summer, if flowering stems are sheared off as soon as they appear in June. Bees are not ideal to sit on! Periwinkle, *Vinca minor*, is also good, clipped at the sides in June. Camomile is quite the most delightful of all, particularly when flowering, but it has to be re-planted annually and cut monthly, and even the non-flowering 'Treneague' lasts only two years before replanting becomes necessary. The seat is brown from October to April and in dry conditions it needs weekly watering. Thymes do well, but they attract too many bees. A plan for a minimum-size brick base is illustrated opposite, but you can use many other dimensions. For instance you may prefer to think of the seat as a low bed of standard sunbed dimensions, or even the width of two sunbeds!

EXEDRA We have already seen that the U-shape or exedra is the neatest way to accommodate a conversing group of people. Drinks and 'finger-food' can be served from a portable table and when it is removed there is space for a couple to recline in the cosy shelter of the U-shape, the seat then doubling as a backrest. The design for an exedra is given below, measuring seven feet six inches by five feet three inches, on which four to six people can sit, with the addition of a portable gar-

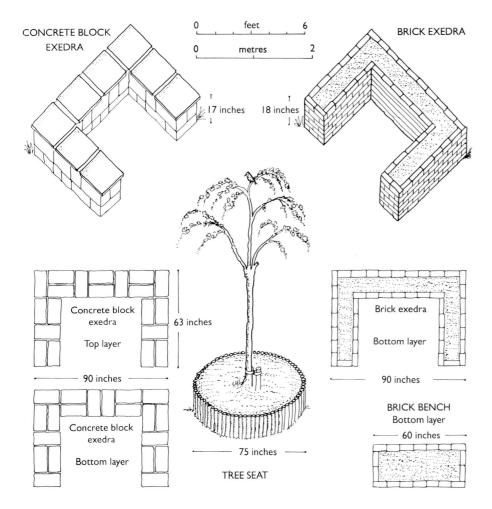

CONCRETE BLOCK EXEDRA

0   feet   6

0   metres   2

BRICK EXEDRA

17 inches

18 inches

Concrete block exedra

Top layer

63 inches

90 inches

Brick exedra

Bottom layer

90 inches

Concrete block exedra

Bottom layer

75 inches

TREE SEAT

BRICK BENCH
Bottom layer

60 inches

Construction drawings for exedra, bench and tree seat.

den table of three by three feet. It can be built with six tiers of brick, but if your 'diy' skills are limited it is easy to construct the base with two tiers of hollow concrete blocks, which are then surfaced with reconstituted stone slabs. Add tubs at the corners if desired. The enclosed U can be turfed, planted with periwinkle, paved or gravelled, but if it is to be turfed, then leave a six-inch mowing strip round the base edges for ease of clipping and strimming.

Materials
Plain brick bench 63 x 18 in, 6 bricks high, requires 108 bricks. Rubble topped up by

9 in of topsoil for the filling.

Brick exedra 90 x 63 in, 6 bricks high (base plan illustrated), requires 252 bricks. Rubble and topsoil filling.

Hollow concrete block exedra 90 x 63 in, two tiers as drawn. 40 blocks (18 x 9 x 9 in, 450 x 225 mm x 225 mm, which includes a mortar allowance). 8 Bradstone pier caps, Hadrian Cotswold. Large size (20½ x 20½ x 2¼ in, 520 x 520 x 60 mm). White masonry paint. Foundation materials (6 in hardcore and 3 in surfacing concrete).

Construction
A manual should be consulted for the method of laying foundations and building in brick and concrete, but the layout of bricks and concrete blocks for the exedra is illustrated here. Note that the surface for the foundation concrete base should be flush with the ground level for brickwork, but should be five inches below ground level for the concrete block exedra so that the blocks can be sunk in order to achieve a final height of about sixteen inches. The concrete blocks should be painted white (the joints can be picked out with rust-red lines as a medieval detail), leaving the stone top unpainted. Four standard recliner chair cushions will exactly fit the top, or can be used in the central U. The large-size Bradstone pier caps have been selected as a good fit for the concrete block exedra, allowing a 1–1½ inch overhang all round without requiring cutting, but other brands may be available.

Flower Borders and Meads

In our present-day borders we underes-

A small trellised herber with a fountain, and an exedra being used as a back-rest. The carnation support would be fixed into holes in the pot rim. French, *c.*1475.

timate the extent to which we rely on long-flowering plants which were not available in medieval Europe but which now help us to achieve a continual flow of form and colour from spring to autumn. Although a medieval list can in theory do the same, the impact is disappointing and it is better to concentrate on a massed effect for brief periods. In the narrow borders of two feet six inches to three feet in width already described for a small trellised herber it is best to plant a row of low aromatic herbs in front of the climbing plants to pick and bruise in the hand whilst sitting. For other beds or borders of four feet or more in width a greater choice of plants is possible, as shown opposite.

Rosemary should be an upright variety, staked, and with the spreading branches trimmed off. Madonna lilies should only be included where the soil is chalky or where a bucket of border soil can be replaced by chalky soil. Sage has the most beautiful flower of all the aromatic herbs and should be cut back after flowering and replaced every third year. The wild dark mullein, *Verbascum nigrum,* treated as a triennial before removal, is better than the gross *Verbascum thapsus.* Sweet rocket is best as a biennial in a border, although for greatest impact it can be kept till its third year in a separate corner where you sit for a summer evening drink, or under a bedroom window. Its perfume is greatest at dawn and dusk and it can form a magnificent bush of about three by three feet or more, too swamping for a border.

A small separate stock area is useful for self-sown plants which cannot easily be bought, or for which you do not have propagating facilities. Two square yards containing one seeding plant of dark mullein, ox-eye daisy and sweet rocket will yield numerous self-sown seedlings for autumn transplanting, and a continuous succession can be kept up in this way. Additional colour can be added by annual 'bedding' plants, and larger numbers of these will be needed to fill the gaps which follow the periodic replanting of the perennials. Useful bedding plants are autumn-planted yellow cowslips (which may last three years), May-planted pot marigolds and *Viola tricolor* (for example, Johnny Jump-Ups). The remaining plants require conventional culture.

A HARDY ANNUAL AREA OF EDIBLE PLANTS, PEAKING IN JUNE
A four-foot wide border can be sown, but the bigger the area the better the effect. A square of about ten by ten feet is ideal, with a cross of one-foot wide paths trampled out on the soil, so that unwanted weeds can be reached. To increase the edible content and to give the patch more structure a permanent plant of rosemary or bay can be positioned centrally, and a border of perennial herbs can be added, including winter savory, thyme, wild marjoram or origan, sage, chives, November-planted greengrocer's garlic (whose green leaves can be eaten), together with ever-ready onions, alpine strawberries, the more authentic but less useful wild strawberries (*Fragaria vesca*), violets and betony.

The new area should be free of

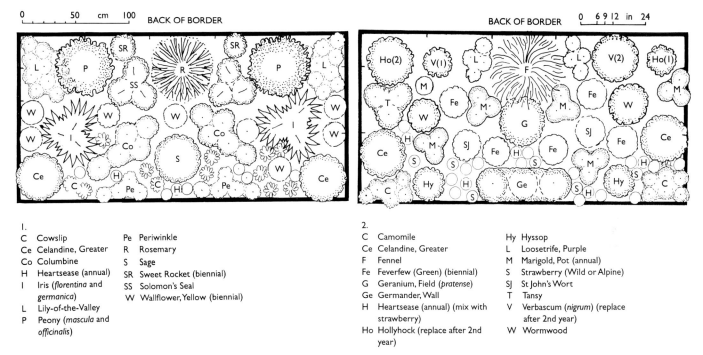

1.

C	Cowslip	Pe	Periwinkle
Ce	Celandine, Greater	R	Rosemary
Co	Columbine	S	Sage
H	Heartsease (annual)	SR	Sweet Rocket (biennial)
I	Iris (*florentina* and *germanica*)	SS	Solomon's Seal
L	Lily-of-the-Valley	W	Wallflower, Yellow (biennial)
P	Peony (*mascula* and *officinalis*)		

2.

C	Camomile	Hy	Hyssop
Ce	Celandine, Greater	L	Loosetrife, Purple
F	Fennel	M	Marigold, Pot (annual)
Fe	Feverfew (Green) (biennial)	S	Strawberry (Wild or Alpine)
G	Geranium, Field (*pratense*)	SJ	St John's Wort
Ge	Germander, Wall	T	Tansy
H	Heartsease (annual) (mix with strawberry)	V	Verbascum (*nigrum*) (replace after 2nd year)
Ho	Hollyhock (replace after 2nd year)	W	Wormwood

Herbaceous border plans for spring and summer.

perennial weeds, dug over in autumn with organic compost incorporated. It should be raked over repeatedly in February and fertilised with a potash-rich dressing such as fish, blood and bone a few weeks before sowing, to achieve a surface suitable for onion seed. Sow mixed seed in drills in the third week in March for June flowering. It is essential to allow plants to seed onto the ground in July and August, shaking them periodically. Inspect the overall composition, and if there has been inadequate germination of any variety then re-sow it the next March. Finally, pull up the seed plants and rake over the surface, pulling out unwanted weeds. Rake and fertilise again the following

February. The floral effect will improve each year and after two or three years when the ground is thoroughly impregnated with seed, it is possible to give it a shallow forking with the addition of compost each autumn. Different plants tend to dominate each year so a balance can be kept by removing excessive ones.

Seeds can be obtained from firms specialising in wild flowers and advice can be given on quantities if you specify your own mixture. Do not expect the initial outlay to be cheap, but subsequent years will be for free. The ideal mixture should contain the following basic species: oats and barley which support the taller species, cornflower, scented mayweed, field poppies, corn

cockle, all of which are in Miriam Rothschild's 'Farmer's Nightmare' mixture. Also add annual violas (and corn marigold for lime-free soil). I like to add rocket, a useful salad annual, whose veined white moth-like flowers add to the effect, pot marigold and garden poppy. Flowers and leaves of these plants, except poppies and corn cockle, can be eaten in soups and salads. If you are not restricted by the need for authenticity, other favourite self-seeding annuals such as love-in-the-mist add to the overall prettiness.

PERENNIAL MEADS The annual area described is a type of annual flowering mead, much more rewarding than try-ing to establish a perennial hay meadow mead which can take up to ten years to perfect. If you wish to brighten up an area of already existing field or orchard turf, one medieval solution is to carve out squares, managed either as above and roughly raked annually; or planted with perennials and newly sown fine turf seed, as described for Sir Roger Vaughan's Garden. The fine display of wild flowers on Prince Charles' estate at Highgrove is a similar mixture of such perennial and annual areas, managed in strips.

A Vine Arbour

The vine was the chief ornamental shade plant not only during the Middle Ages but up until the eighteenth century when it was ousted by more floriferous climbers. These days a vine arbour can add a touch of Mediterranean atmosphere to an *al fresco* meal, and can produce passable outdoor dessert grapes. The arbour should be situated in a sunny spot, but it should not be a focal point in the garden since vines do not look ornamental from October to May. Vines need support because they are floppy rather than heavy, and any structure which can carry roses is suitable, including a simple single metal arch. However a wooden arbour whose roof is crossed by bars about two feet apart will finally look more medieval than will a commercial metal frame, since you cannot rely on low vine growth to conceal the corner poles.

A jointed structure of four- to six-inches diameter square-cut oak timber is the most handsome and durable, but a rustic framework echoes what was more common in medieval gardens. However this too will have to be jointed rather than using medieval-style forked corner poles which are only formed in hardwood trees, and are now virtually unobtainable commercially. On the continent one often sees the flimsiest of arbours with bamboo-frame roofs tied to four corner posts, and this could be used too if the idea of the arbour is more important to you than is authenticity. The height of the arbour should be about seven feet six inches with eighteen inches of extra pole length below ground, and the vines can be pruned by ladder.

Materials for a nine- by seven-foot arbour
Tanalized soft wood poles (allowing for 6 in overhang):
4 poles, 9ft x 4in, for uprights
2 poles, 10ft x 3-4in, for front and back
6 poles, 8ft x 3-4in, for cross bars
Galvanized nails, hardcore and concrete, 4 vines.

THE VINES One vine will be necessary for a six-foot arbour, depending on the variety, with roses or cucumbers growing on the other two posts if you wish. A vine at each of the four corners will be necessary for a larger structure. For dessert grapes the best varieties are the black Tereshkova and the white Madeline Sylvaner. The vigorous Brant has beautiful red autumn colouring with miniature bunches of sweet black grapes which appeal to children, but is American in origin, and therefore not medieval. Wrotham Pinot has a very handsome dusky grey leaf and is very vigorous if you require black grapes for wine. Obtain bare-rooted one-year old plants, by mail from a specialist grower rather than older potted garden centre plants and do not be afraid to ask for adequate planting instructions.

CULTIVATION A vine is simple to cultivate if you become its master in the first year, starting with a bare-rooted cutting which has three or four buds. By planting in March, the aim is to grow one 'trunk' to the height of the roof in the first summer, tying it in and cutting back to three leaves any other shoots that grow. If the height is not reached in the first year do not hesitate to cut the newly grown shoot back to three buds in November, almost to ground, and start again, remembering that in the end your vine will outlive you. Give it a gallon of water a day for the first two summers to ensure strong roots. In the winter after the full height has been achieved stop the trunk at roof height, and leave three buds at the top, rubbing out all others down the trunk. From these allow two branches to grow across the arbour roof, tying them in. If there are several vines arrange these branches to grow across the top, parallel to each other. The buds which show on these by the end of the year will be about one foot apart and will be the site of all future grape-producing spurs. Let all these buds grow and you will be delighted to see that each produces several bunches of flowers, only one bunch being kept to develop grapes, and the others cut off, on each spur shoot. In the winter cut all these spur shoots back to about one inch, leaving two to three buds to produce the next years' grape-bearing shoots. In May or early June let only one shoot per spur develop fully, rubbing the others out.

For grapes, the grape-bearing shoot itself can be shortened to two leaves beyond the grape bunch, but remember that you may prefer to leave the greenery to provide shade. If only one shoot at each spur does not give enough summer shade, then the next year leave two at each. Increasingly knotty spurs will gradually form in years to come as you repeat this harsh pruning in winter. Any fertiliser recommended for roses or gooseberries will suit vines. The simple overall principle should be in the back of your mind when pruning, once your spur framework is built up: cut all the current year's growth back to two or three buds.

A Tree Seat

Seats were commonly made round the base of trees, the built up soil being supported by wattle or a stone wall. As the former is short-lived and the latter expensive a practical alternative is a wall of chestnut poles. The chosen area should be well prepared for tree planting, in autumn or early spring, by breaking up the soil to about twelve inches in depth and about three feet in diameter. Put a stick to mark the centre, and then draw a circle about six feet in diameter (using a string as the radius). Run a line of sand along the circle circumference for better visibility. Then drive chestnut posts along the sand line as close to each other as possible, allowing a height of about sixteen inches above ground level, using a wooden mallet or beetle so as not to

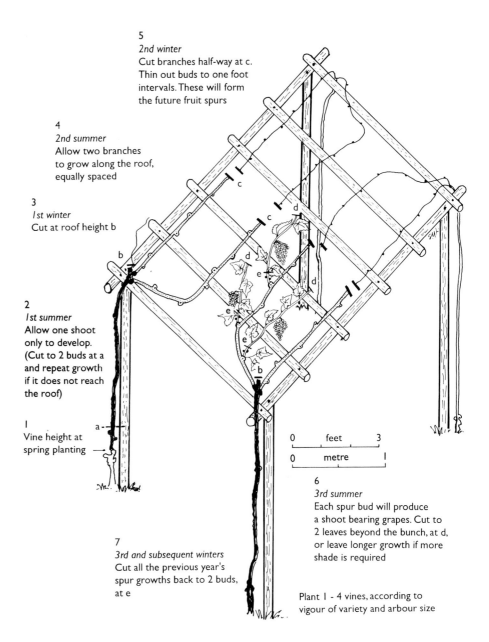

5
2nd winter
Cut branches half-way at c. Thin out buds to one foot intervals. These will form the future fruit spurs

4
2nd summer
Allow two branches to grow along the roof, equally spaced

3
1st winter
Cut at roof height b

2
1st summer
Allow one shoot only to develop. (Cut to 2 buds at a and repeat growth if it does not reach the roof)

1
Vine height at spring planting

0   feet   3
0   metre   1

6
3rd summer
Each spur bud will produce a shoot bearing grapes. Cut to 2 leaves beyond the bunch, at d, or leave longer growth if more shade is required

Plant 1 - 4 vines, according to vigour of variety and arbour size

7
3rd and subsequent winters
Cut all the previous year's spur growths back to 2 buds, at e

Vine arbour, showing method of vine pruning.

A small vine arbour of forked poles, with a single vine, branched from the base. Grapes are being trampled in the barrel to make wine. 15th century.

or a friend already have a periwinkle patch elsewhere which needs to be dug up it is worth spreading a few inches of soil over it after flowering. Let the runners root into it and transplant pieces in the autumn.

My choice of tree would be a Glastonbury thorn, *Crataegus monogyna* var. *biflora*, for which there may be a waiting list. Its dainty leaves and form, pink flowers, berries, ability to withstand a raised position and to suffer pruning to a neat umbrella shape, make it the best authentic choice. Other present-day species of *Crataegus* are equally suitable where authenticity is not essential.

You may not want to risk building a seat round an already existing healthy tree, but if you have an ailing one of any type, with only a few years of life left, then such a seat can be built round it, in which a climbing rose can be grown, tied to the trunk. Although not authentically medieval a vigorous rose such as Rambling Rector or Wedding Day can be chosen to add a last few years of beauty.

Materials

Chestnut poles, from a fencing firm, 3in diameter, 25-27in long, flat-topped and pointed ends. Pressure tanalized (brown) to preserve. 85 posts for a 6ft diameter seat will give a few spare ones.

Tree of your choice, but a 6ft standard is required.

Periwinkle: 100 plants (3½-in pots)

Topsoil: Approximately 5 cu yds. 3ft stake.

split the tops. (Lubrication with cow manure will assist the driving in!)

Line the post ring side internally with black plastic, which has a few holes in it, to stop soil working through. The ring should then be half filled with chopped turves, soil and well-rotted compost, to which fertiliser should be added to the central three feet. A three-foot tree support should then be driven into the ring ground, slightly off-centre, protruding one foot above the seat level. Plant the six-foot standard tree centrally so that its trunk base is

about six inches below seat level, tying it to the stake and adding and compacting the soil as you work, removing the post in a year's time. There is inevitably a drop in level of about 3–4 inches in the following months so leave the soil level a few inches above the perimeter post level.

The seat surface should be planted with dwarf periwinkle, *Vinca minor*, which is completely durable for sitting on, planting from 3½-inch pots at 6-inch intervals. This will soon form a matted cushion, but to economise, if you

Places to Visit

(If travelling from some distance it is wise to confirm opening times.)

RE-CREATED GARDENS

All of the re-created gardens are at their best from May to July. Although they are unique as prototype medieval gardens, they are small and therefore best visited as part of a more extended tour.

ENGLAND

Bayleaf, Weald and Downland Museum (details below). A homestead associated with a fifteenth-century Kentish yeoman's house. Orchard, croft, shaw hedge and re-created vegetable and herb garden. 90 x 100 feet. (The whole complex was designed by a research team, directed by Christopher Zeuner. Garden designed by Sylvia Landsberg, with John Harvey as consultant.) Illustrated booklet. S.A.E. for details.

Hangleton, Weald and Downland Museum (details below). An example of a thirteenth-century retired couple's garden, as could have existed within a larger close. 26 x 24 feet. (In process of construction – designer Sylvia Landsberg.)

Queen Eleanor's Garden, Great Hall, The Castle, Winchester, Hants (01962) 840476. 10 a.m.–5 p.m. Every day except Christmas and Boxing Day. A late thirteenth-century re-creation of a royal castle herber. A narrow triangle of 30 x 90 feet. Illustrated leaflet and plant list from County Secretary, The Castle, Winchester. S.A.E. for details. (Designer Sylvia Landsberg, co-designer John Harvey, for Hampshire County Council.)

The Shrewsbury Quest, 193 Abbey Foregate, Shrewsbury, Shropshire S42 6AH (01743) 366355. Open daily 10 a.m. till dusk (or 5.30 p.m.) except Christmas Day and New Year's Day. A centre relating to the fictitious monastery herbalist, Brother Cadfael, of Ellis Peters' novels. Features of monastic gardens are displayed within a cloistered area 90 x 90 feet: twelfth-century physician's garden; fourteenth-century abbot's herber; additional features and utilitarian plants. (Designer Sylvia Landsberg; consultant John Harvey.)

Sir Roger Vaughan's Garden, Tretower Court, Tretower, Crickhowell, Powys (01874) 730279. 9.30 a.m.–6 p.m., in summer, to 3.30 p.m. in winter. Sundays 2 p.m.–6 p.m. A late fifteenth-century nobleman's garden. Area 60 x 100 feet. Illustrated leaflet and plant list. S.A.E. for details. (Designer Elisabeth Whittle, for Cadw.)

The Tudor Garden, St Michael's Square, Bugle Street, Southampton, Hants SO14 2AD (01703) 332513. 10 a.m.–12.00 and 1 p.m.–5 p.m., Tuesday-Friday (4 p.m. Saturday); 2 p.m.–5 p.m. Sunday. (Phone before making a special journey.) 60 x 70 feet. A sixteenth-century garden with many medieval plants and some medieval features (1485-1603). (Designer Sylvia Landsberg, for Southampton City Council.)

The Weald and Downland Open Air Museum, Singleton, Chichester, West Sussex, PO18 0EU (01243) 811348. March-October, daily; November-February, Wednesdays, Sundays and Bank Holiday Mondays 10 a.m.–5 p.m. Originally a centre for the rescue of vernacular buildings, but in addition many country crafts are demonstrated.

FRANCE

Fontevraud Abbey. Centre Culturel de l'Ouest, Abbaye Royale de Fontevraud, 49590 Fontevraud – L'Abbaye. The best monastic herb and vegetable garden re-creation. (Designer Michel Cambornac, consultant Dr. C. Mathon.)

Le Jardin Carolingien, Service des Espaces Verts, Ville de Melle, Deux-Sèvres. A ninth-century re-created garden of plants listed in the time of Charlemagne. (Researcher Dr. C. Mathon.)

U.S.A.

The Cloisters Museum, Fort Tryon Park, N.Y. 10040. Planted as a secular cloister, containing beds of medieval plants (monastic cloisters were not planted up). (Designer Susan Moody.)

PRIORIES AND CASTLES

Gardens can be imagined in walled areas of many monastic and castle ruins; however the following sites are outstanding.

Christ Church Priory, Canterbury. The main cloister garth still exists, also the site of the infirmary cloister garth and herbarium. The twelfth-century lead water pipe still lies 15 inches below ground, running along the south side of Military Road. (See illustration on p. 42.)

Bodiam Castle, Bodiam, E. Sussex. Open mid-February – Christmas, daily 10 a.m. – dusk, or 6 p.m. A fifteenth-century moated castle (see illustration p. 9.)

Leeds Castle, near Maidstone, Kent ME17 1PL (01622) 765400 (4 miles east of Maidstone, off M20, Junction 8). Open daily except Christmas Day. March–October 10 a.m.–5 p.m.; November–February 10 a.m.–3 p.m. (closed June 25, July 2, November 5). A favourite castle of royalty since the reign of Edward I. The surrounding Capability Brown Park gives the feel of a medieval park.

MISCELLANEOUS FEATURES

COPPICES

Bradfield Woods, Bradfield St George, Suffolk (3 miles S.E. of Bury St Edmunds, between Bradfield St George and Felsham. Map ref. TL935581). Open daily. Visitor centre open Sundays and Bank Holiday Mondays, Easter to September. National Nature Reserve, managed by medieval methods since 1252.)

Weald and Downland Museum. See above.

(Other, local examples, nationwide.)

DOVECOT

Basing House, Basing, Hants (01256) 467294. Seventeenth-century dovecot but with doves and central revolving ladder demonstrating the medieval principle.

FISH STORAGE POND, OR *SERVATORIUM*

St Cross Hospital, St Cross, Winchester, Hants. Open daily. (Position of possible moated orchard is also visible here.)

FLOWERING MEADS

Near Peterborough, managed by the Hon. Miriam Rothschild. Phone in office hours for best visiting dates. Ashton Farm Partners, Ashton Estate Office, Ashton, Peterborough PE8 5LE (01832) 272675.

North Meadow Nature Reserve, Cricklade, Wilts (entrance off A419 junction of A419 and B4040). Lammas land, still farmed by the medieval practice of common grazing pasture from Lammas to Lady Day (August 12–February 12) and then grown as hay during summer. Open land; public access is via pathways across the site; best period late April–mid-June. For parties, contact English Nature, Devizes (01380) 726344.

A TRYSTING PLACE

Rosamund's Bower, Everswell, Blenheim Palace (see illustration p.21). Only one pool survives, at the edge of Capability Brown's lake, but water has continued to fill it since the twelfth century.

MATERIALS

Unboiled willow rods (with bark). The English Basket and Hurdle Centre, Curload, Stoke St-Gregory, Taunton, Somerset TA3 6JD.

Oak lath. Approx. 1¼ in x 4 ft. Available from local wood-men, or Carpenter Oak and Woodland Ltd, Hall Farm, Thickwood Lane, Colerne, Chippenham, Wilts SN14 8BE.

Coppiced hazel and chestnut poles and oak lath. Forestry Commission or local woodmen.

Wild flower seeds and plants. Available from many firms advertised in specialist books and magazines, but the Hon. Miriam Rothschild provides purely British seed, a range of hedgerow plants, and helpful advice (see address above).

Small quantities of cane can be bought from a local basket maker, or by mail order from The Cane Shop, 207 Blackstock Road, Highbury Vale, London N5 2LL 0171 354 4210.

*B*ibliography

BACKGROUND READING

Amherst, A., 1896, *A History of Gardening in England*, Quarritch (facsimile edn., 1969, Singing Tree Press, Detroit)

Crisp, Sir F.,1966, *Mediaeval Gardens*, Hacker, New York (reprint 1979)

Harvey, J. H., 1981, *Mediaeval Gardens*, Batsford, London (paperback edn. 1990)

Harvey, J. H., 1988, *Restoring Period Gardens*, Shire Publications Ltd, Aylesbury (2nd edn. 1993)

Jellicoe, J., et al., eds, 1986, *Oxford Companion to Gardens*, Oxford University Press, Oxford (several articles on medieval gardens)

McDougall, E. B., ed., 1986, *Medieval Gardens*, Dumbarton Oaks Colloquium on the History of Landscape Architecture IX, Harvard University

McLean, T., 1981, *Medieval English Gardens*, Collins, London (2nd edn. 1994)

Peplow, E. and R., 1988, *In a Monastery Garden*, David and Charles, London

Stokstad, M., and Stannard, J., 1983, *Gardens of the Middle Ages* (ex. cat.) University of Kansas

REFERENCES

Aberg, F. A., ed., 1978, *Medieval Moated Sites*, Council for British Archaeology, Research Report no. 17, London

Aston, M., 1970-2, 'Earthworks at the Bishop's Palace, Alvechurch, Worcestershire', *Transactions of the Worcestershire Archaeological Society* 3, Ser 3, pp. 55-9

Aston, M., ed., 1988, Medieval Fish, Fisheries and Fishponds in England, B.A.R. British Series 182, (i), (ii), Oxford

Beresford, M., Hurst, J., 1990, *Wharram Percy Deserted Medieval Village*, Batsford/English Heritage, London

Braunfels, W., 1972, *Monasteries of Western Europe*, Thames and Hudson, London

Brereton, G. E., Ferrier, J. M., eds., 1981, *Le Menagier de Paris*, Clarendon Press, Oxford

Butler, H. E., ed., 1949 *The Chronicle of Jocelin of Brakelond*, Medieval Classics, London

Calkins, R. G., 1986, 'Piero de' Crescenzi and the Medieval Garden', in McDougall. E. B., 1986, above

Cantor, L., 1983, *The Medieval Parks of England - A Gazetteer*, University of Loughborough

Colvin, H., ed., 1963, *History of the King's Works*, H.M.S.O., London

Coppack, G., 1990, *Abbeys and Priories*, Batsford/English Heritage, London

Currie, C. K., 1988, 'Hampshire Medieval Fishponds' in Aston, M., ed., 1988, above

Currie, C. K., 1990, 'Fishponds as Garden Features *c*. 1550-1750', *Garden History*, 18 no. 1, pp. 22-46

Currie, C. K., 1992, 'St Cross: A medieval moated garden?', Hampshire Gardens Trust Journal 11, pp. 19-22.

Hampshire Printing Services, Winchester

Davis, A. H. (trans.), 1934, *William Thorne's Chronicle of St Augustine's Abbey, Canterbury*, Blackwell, Oxford

Dawson, W. R., 1934, *A Leechbook or Collection of Medical Recipes of the Fifteenth Century*, Macmillan & Co. Ltd, London

de Boer, G., 1973, 'The two earliest Maps of Hull', *Post-Medieval Archaeology*, 7, p. 79

Dickie, J., 1981, 'The Islamic Garden in Spain', *The Islamic Garden*, Mcdougall E. B., Ettinghausen, R. E., eds., Dumbarton Oaks Colloquium on the History of Landscape Architecture, IV, Harvard University

Eco, U., 1986, *Art and Beauty in the Middle Ages*, Vale University Press, New Haven and London

Everson, P., 1991, 'Field Survey and Garden Earthworks', *Garden Archaeology*, ed. Brown, A. E., Council for British Archaeology, Research Report no. 78, pp. 6-19

Everson, P. L., Taylor, C. C., Dunn, C. J., 1991, *Change and Continuity: rural settlement in N.W. Lincolnshire*, H.M.S.O., London

Fitzherbert, Master, 1534, 'The Booke of Husbandrie', ed. Skeat, W. W., *English Dialect Society*, 1882, London

Hanawalt, B., 1986, *The Ties That Bound*, Oxford University Press, New York

Harvey, J.H., 1981, see above under 'Background Reading'

Harvey, J. H., 1982, *Garden History Society*, Newsletter 5

Harvey, J. H., 1984, 'Vegetables in the Middle Ages', *Garden History*, 12 no. 2, pp. 91-9

Harvey, J. H., 1985, 'The First English Garden Book: Mayster Jon Gardener's Treatise and its Background', *Garden History*, 13 no. 2, pp. 83-101

Harvey, J. H., 1987, "The Square Garden of Henry the Poet', *Garden History*, 15 no. 1, pp. 1-11

Harvey, J. H., 1987, 'Henry Daniel: a Scientific Gardener of the 14th century', *Garden History*, 15 no. 2, pp. 81-93

Harvey, J. H., 1989, 'Garden Plants of around 1525', The Fromond List, *Garden History*, 17 no. 2, pp. 122-134

Harvey, J. H., 1992, 'Westminster Abbey: The Infirmarer's Garden', Garden History, 20 no. 2, pp. 1-97

Harvey, J. H., 1994, 'Gardening in the Age of Chaucer' in 'Symposium - Plants and People AD 800-1800', *Botanical Journal of Scotland*, Vol. 46, pt. 4., pp. 564-573

Harvey, P. D. A., 1965, A *Medieval Oxfordshire Village - Cuxham*, Oxford University Press, Oxford

Hockey, S. F., ed., 1965, *Beaulieu Abbey Accounts*, Camden 4th Series, 16, Royal Historical Society, London

Holden, E. W., 1963, 'Excavations at the Deserted Medieval Village of Hangleton, Pt 1', *Sussex Archaeological Collections*, Vol. 101, pp. 54-181

Horn, W., Born, E., 1979, *The Plan of St Gall*, 3 Vols. University of California Press, Berkeley

Horrox, R., 1978, *The Changing Plan of Hull 1290-1650*, Kingston upon Hull City Council

Landsberg, S., 1995, 'The Re-creation of Small Period

Gardens for Museums and Public Spaces in Britain', *Museum Management and Curatorship*, Vol. 14 no. 4

Landsberg, S., 1996, 'Bayleaf - a medieval yeoman's garden', *The Garden*, Vol. 121 no. 6

Liveing, H. G. D., 1906, *Records of Romsey Abbey*, Warren and Son

'Macer', ed. G. Frisk, 1949, *A Middle English translation of Macer Floridus De Viribus Herbarum*, Upsala

Moorehouse, S. A., 1991, 'Ceramics in the Medieval Garden', *Garden Archaeology*, ed. Brown, A. E., *Council for British Archaeology*, Research Report no. 78, p. 100

Mountain, D. (Thomas Hill), 1577, *The Gardeners Labyrinth* (facsimile 1982, Garland Publishing Inc., New York, London)

Opsomer-Halleux, C., 1986, 'The Medieval Garden and its Role in Medicine', in McDougall, E. B., 1986, above

Oschinsky, D., 1971, *Walter of Henley and other Treatises on Estate Management*, Clarendon Press, Oxford

Paul, M., 1985, 'Turf Seats in French Gardens of the Middle Ages', *Journal of Garden History*, Vol. 5, no. 1, pp. 3-14

Payne, R., Blunt, W., 1966, *Hortulus*, The Hunt Botanical Library, Pittsburgh

Pearsall, D., ed., 1962, *The Floure and the Leafe*, Nelson and Sons Ltd., London

Power, E., 1928, *The Goodman of Paris* (partial translation of *Le Menagier de Paris*), Routledge and Sons Ltd., London

Rackham, O., 1986, *History of the Countryside*, J. M. Dent

and Son Ltd.

Rowland, B., 1981, *Medieval Woman's Guide to Health* (MS Sloane 2463) Croom Helm, London

Smith, R. M., 'Rooms, Relatives and Residential Arrangements 1250-1500', *Medieval Village Research Group*, Annual Report 30, p. 34

Stearn, W., 1943, 'The Welsh Onion and the Everready Onion', *The Gardener's Chronicle*, Sept. 4, pp. 86-88

Tabbana, J. G. H., 1987, 'Towards an Interpretation of the Use of Water in Islamic Courtyards', *Journal of Garden History*, Vol. 7, no. 3, pp. 197-220

Taylor, C. C., 1989, 'Somersham Palace, Cambridgeshire: A Medieval Landscape for Pleasure?', *From Cornwall to Caithness*, Bowden, M., Mackay, D., Topping, P., eds, B.A.R., British Series 209, Oxford

Taylor, C., Everson, P., Wilson-North, R., 1990, 'Bodiam Castle, Sussex', *Medieval Archaeology*, 34, pp. 153-156

Thompson, M. W., 1964, 'Reclamation of Waste Ground for the Pleasance of Kenilworth Castle, Warwickshire', *Medieval Archaeology*, 8, pp. 222-3

Thompson, M. W., 1991, *The Rise of the Castle*, Cambridge University Press, Cambridge

Titow, J. Z., 1969, *English Rural Society 1200-1350*, Allen & Unwin, London

Trevisa, John, 1399, *On the Properties of Things*, trans. of Bartholomaeus Angelicus, *De Proprietatibus Rerum* (ed. M. C. Seymour, Clarendon Press, Oxford, 1975, 2 vols)

Tusser, T., 1580, *Five*

Hundred Points of Good Husbandry (Oxford University Press, Oxford, 1984)

Urry, W., 1967, *Canterbury under the Angevin Kings*, Athlone Press, London

Van Buren, A. H., 1986, 'The Park at Hesdin', *Medieval Gardens*, in McDougall, E. B., 1986, above

Virgoe, R., 1989, *Illustrated Letters of the Paston Family*, Macmillan, London

Waddell, H., 1949, *The Wandering Scholars*, Constable, London

Whittle, E., 1989, 'The Renaissance Gardens of Reglan Castle', *Garden History*, 17 no. 2, pp. 83-94

Willis, D., ed., 1916, *The Estate Book of Henry de Bray*, Camden 3rd series, 27, Royal Historical Society, London

Acknowledgements

I have had the opportunity to explore the reality of medieval gardens more than many others have been able to do, because I have followed in the footsteps of a leading architectural and garden historian, who has worked on medieval gardens over a period of some forty years. John Harvey's work on the subject is available for all to read, but I have had the additional privilege of his generous assistance, by correspondence and by conversation, in the re-creation of gardens. He is the co-designer of Queen Eleanor's Garden and consultant for Bayleaf and The Shrewsbury Quest gardens. He has also allowed me to quote passages from his published work.

Others who have explored the process of re-creation with me have also thereby contributed to this book: Brian Grayling, the architect and 'enabler' of Queen Eleanor's Garden; Bob Holman and Graham Cox who constructed and still maintain the Bayleaf and Shrewsbury Quest gardens, respectively; and also the craftsmen and gardeners, Peter Wheble, Graham Garner, Adrian Crook and Peter Prior.

Prof. Colin Platt has continually encouraged the growth of this book and has made valuable comments; Maggie Black found a publisher; Chris Currie introduced me to important archaeological developments; Dorothy Barkley and Diana Landsberg read the MS and made many helpful remarks.

Mike Aston (pp. 68, 72), James Bond (p. 104), P. D. A. Harvey (pp. 26, 32), and Elisabeth Whittle (p. 119) have allowed me to use, copy, or even add to their illustrations. Mrs K. Urry has kindly allowed me to use research details of the late W. Urry (p. 42). Maureen Pemberton and Louise Gittings have been of particular help in the search for pictures. Many others have assisted me, including Geraldine Angel, Richard Barkley, Paul Bennett of the Kent Archaeological Trust, Paul Cattermole, Lorne Campbell, Susan Campbell, the late Ruth Duthie, Sheila Fordham, John Hurst, Olivia Landsberg, Peter Matthews, John Steane and Lore Worth. Sue Hayter and Pat Wood typed the manuscript.

Confidence-inspiring

Sarah Derry of the British Museum Press has pruned the text and tied in loose ends, latterly most nobly followed by Colin Grant. And always in the background there has been the unending forbearance of my husband, Peter. In this cramped space I cannot adequately do justice to you all. Many thanks for your help.

Permission has kindly been granted to quote the extracts on the following pages from the publications cited: 11 Tony Conran, *Welsh Verse*, Seren, Bridgend, 1986; 12 M.W. Thompson, 'Reclamation of Waste Ground for the Pleasance of Kenilworth Castle', *Medieval Archaeology*, 8, 1964, pp. 222-3; 26 John Trevisa, *On the Properties of Things*, 1399 (trens. of Bartholomaeus Angelicus, *De Proprietatibus Rerum*), ed. M.C. Seymour, Clarendon Press, Oxford, 1975, by permission of Oxford University Press; 37-8, 97 (below) and 99-100 Walahfrid Strabo, *De Cultura Hortulorum*, trans. R. Payne, Hunt Botanical Library, Pittsburgh, 1966; 83 B. Rowland, *Medieval Woman's Guide to Health*, Croom Helm, London, 1981; 97 and 116 Thomas Tusser, *Five Hundred Points of Good Husbandry* (1580), 1984, by permission of Oxford University Press.

Index of Plants

The following serves both as a list of the common and Latin names of the plants and trees that have been grown in the re-created gardens discussed here, and as an index to those that are given more than a passing mention in the text. For convenience of comparison the names are mainly those as identified by John Harvey (Harvey 1981, 1985, 1989), which are based on the R.H.S. *Dictionary of Gardening*, 1956/65. Page numbers in italics (placed after the text references) indicate illustrations.

* self-seeding 'edible weeds' in vegetable beds.

HERBACEOUS PLANTS
AND SHRUBS

Agrimony (*Agrimonia eupatoria*) 79

Alexanders or Stanmarch (*Smyrnium olusatrum*) 79, 83, 112, 113

Balm (*Melissa officinalis*)

Bay, Sweet (*Laurus nobilis*) 80, 121, *82*

Bean, Broad (*Vicia faba*) *18*, 76

Beet, Leaf (*Beta vulgaris*) 28, 79, 118

Betony (*Betonica officinalis*) 79, 83, 102, 112, 120, *82*

Bluebell (*Endymion nonscriptus*) 81, *107*

Borage (*Borago officinalis*) 58, 79, *82*

Box (*Buxus sempervirens*) *3, 6*

Broom (*Sarothamnus scoparius*) 81, *125*

Bryony, White (*Bryonia dioica*) 102

Bugle (*Ajuga reptans*) 80

Bugloss (*Anchusa officinalis*) 76

Camomile (*Chamaemelum nobile*) 112, 120, 131, *82*

*Camomile, Wild, or Scented Mayweed (*Matricaria recutita*) 58, 113

Campion, Red (*Melandrium dioicum*) 80, 119

Campion, White (*M. album*) 113

Carnation, *see* Pink

Catmint or Nepp (*Nepeta cataria*) 79

Celandine, Greater (*Chelidonium majus*) 81, 126, *back cover*

Celery, Smallage or Celery Leaf (*Apium graveolens*) 80

Chervil (*Anthriscus cerefolium*) 79

*Chickweed (*Stellaria media*) 80, 84, *30*

Chicory or Succory (*Cichorium intybus*) 83

Chives (*Allium schoenoprasum*) 28, 79, *82*

Cockle, Corn (*Agrostemma githago*) 58, 78

Colewort or Kale (*Brassica oleracea*) 28, 48, 77, 79, 97, 117, *118*

Columbine (*Aquilegia vulgaris*) 79, 80, 104, 119, 124, 126, *18*

Comfrey (*Symphytum officinale*) 74, 81, 112

Coriander (*Coriandrum sativum*) 79

Cornflower (*Centaurea cyanus*) 58, 119, *76*

Cowslip (*Primula veris*) 58, 81, 134

Cress, Garden (*Lepidium sativum*) 80

*Cress of Boleyn or French (American) Cress (*Barbarea vulgaris*) 80

Daisy, Common (*Bellis perennis*) 74, 79, *6, 76, 78,* 127

Daisy, Ox-eye (*Chrysanthemum leucanthemum*) 74, 134, *82*

*Dandelion (*Taraxacum officinale*) 79, *30*

Dill (*Peucedanum graveolens*) 79, 113

Dyer's Greenweed (*Genista tinctoria*) 104

Elecampane (*Inula helenium*) 80, 104

*Fat Hen (*Chenopodium album*) *see* Orach

Fennel (*Foeniculum vulgare*) 31, 79, 83, 102, 112, 113, 116, 127, *82*

Fern, Female (*Athyrium filix-femina*) 81, 126, *back cover*

Fern, Male (*Dryopteris filix-mas*) 81, *62*

*Feverfew (*Chrysanthemum parthenium*) 81, 113

Flax (*Linum usitatissimum*) 28, 46

Foxglove (*Digitalis purpurea* and *alba*) 81, 120

Garlic (*Allium sativum*) 28, 76, 80

*Garlic Mustard or Sauce Alone (*Alliaria petiolata*) 81, 119

Germander (*Teucrium chamaedrys*) 80, 112, *82*

*Good King Henry (*Chenopodium bonus-henricus*) 79, 112

Gourd (*Lagenaria vulgaris*) 50, 80

*Groundsel (*Senecio vulgaris*) 31, 84

Guelder Rose (*Viburnum opulus*) 81

Hartstongue (*Phyllitis scolopendrium*) 79, *82*

Hawthorn (*Crataegus monogyna*) 65, 125, *front cover, 64*

Hazel (*Corylus avellana*) 61, 66, 106, 62, 107

Heartsease (*Viola tricolor*) 76, 80, 124, 134, *76, 78, 82*

Hellebore (*Helleborus niger* or *viridis*) 80

Henbane (*Hyoscyamus niger*) 80

Hollyhock (*Althaea rosea*) 76, 104, 126

Honeysuckle or Woodbine (*Lonicera periclymenum*) 50, 65, 104, 118, 119, 124

Horehound, White (*Marrubium vulgare*) 112, 116

Hyssop (*Hyssopus officinalis*) 28, 80, 104, 116, 117, 127, 131, *82, 115*

Iris, Gladdon (*Iris foetidissima*) 126, *back cover*

Iris, Purple (*I. germanica*) 81, 124, *82*

Iris, White (*I. florentina*) 81, 124

Ivy (*Hedera helix*) 50, 122, *126, 127*

*Langdebeef (*Picris echioides*) 31, 79

Lavender (*Lavandula spica*) 76, 81, 104, 126, 132, *82*

Leek (*Allium porrum*) 28, 77, 79, 84, 97, 116, 117, *30, 91*

Lily, Madonna (*Lilium candidum*) 80, 104, 112, 124, *3, 78*

Lily of the Valley (*Convallaria majalis*) 80, 119

Loosetrife, Purple (*Lythrum salicaria*)

Lovage (*Levisticum officinale*) 31, 80, 112

Madder (*Rubia tinctorum*) 104

*Mallow, Common (*Malva sylvestris*) 31, 79

Mandrake (*Mandragora officinarum*) 80

Marigold, Corn (*Chrysanthemum segetum*) 58, 81

Marigold, Pot (*Calendula officinalis*) 58, 79, 83, 113, 134, *82, 115*

Mint (*Mentha* spp.) 31, 43, 79, 84, 112, 116, *82*

Monkshood (*Aconitum napellus*) 102

Mugwort (*Artemisia vulgaris*) 80, 84, 116

Mullein (*Verbascum nigrum* and *thapsus*) 134

Mustard (*Sinapis alba*)

*Nettle, Red (*Lamium purpureum*) 31, 79, *30*

Nightshade, Black (*Solanum nigrum*)

Onion, Bulb (*Allium cepa*) 28, 77, 80, 97

Onion, Ever-ready (*Allium cepa* var. *perutile*) 28, 77, 112, 117

*Orach (*Atriplex*, *Chenopodium* spp.) 79, *30*

Origan or Wild Marjoram (*Origanum vulgare*) 79, *82*

Parsley, Plain-leaved (*Petroselinum crispum*) 28, 76, 79, 83, 84, 113, 117

Parsnip (*Peucedanum sativum*) 28, 77, 80

Pea (*Pisum sativum*) 77

Pennyroyal (*Mentha pulegium*) 31, 80, 112, *82*

Peony, Roman (*Paeonia officinalis*) 80, 122

Peony, Male (*P. mascula*) 122, *75*

Periwinkle (*Vinca minor*) 80, 105, 126, 131, *78*

*Pimpernel, Scarlet (*Anagallis arvensis*) 31, *30*

Pink or Carnation (*Dianthus caryophyllus*) 80, 127, *front cover, 15, 76, 78, 105*

*Plantain, Ribwort (*Plantago lanceolata*) 31, 81

*Plantain, Waybread (*P. major*) 31, 81, *30*

Polypody (*Polypodium vulgare*) 81, *82*

Poppy, Corn (*Papaver rhoeas*) 58

Poppy, Garden (*P. somniferum*) 58, 80, 102, *82, 107*

Primrose (*Primula vulgaris*) 61, 80, 126

Radish (*Raphanus sativus*) 79

Rape (*Brassica napus*) 79

Rocket (*Eruca sativa*) 80, *82*

Rocket, Sweet (*Hesperis matronalis*) 81, 134, *78*

Rose, Burnet (*Rosa spinosissima* or *pimpinellifolia*)

Rose, Field (*R. arvensis*)

Rose, Red (*R. gallica* var. *officinalis*) 50, 80, 104, 119, 125, *front cover, 6, 75, 76, 78, 126*

Rose, Sweet Briar (*R. rubiginosa* or *eglanteria*) 65, 104, 118, 125

Rose, White (*R. x alba* var. *semi-plena*) 50, 119, 125,

Illustration Credits

Illustrations and/or permission to reproduce them have kindly been provided by the following:
A K G, London: 75 (Martin Schongauer, *Madonna im Rosenhag*); M. Aston (redrawn from): 68, 72; Bibliotheca Philosophica Hermetica (*Hours of Albrecht of Brandenburg*): 3 (f.59v), 75 (f.9); Bibliothèque de l'Arsenal: 134 (MS Arsenal 5072, f.71v); Bibliothèque Nationale, Paris: 8 (MS fr 19153, f.7), 18 (MS fr 143, f.198v), 19 (MS fr 12330, f.105r), 50 (MS Arsenal 5070, f.168), 90 (MS Arsenal 5064, f.151v); Bibliothèque Royale, Brussels: 60 (MS 9392, f.41v); J. Bond: 104; Bridgeman Art Library: 99 (de Sphaera, *Mercury* - Biblioteca Estense, Modena), 138 (Bibliothèque Nationale, Paris, NAL 1673, f.103v); British Library: 6 (Harley MS 4425, f.12v), 17 (Harley MS 4375, f.151v), 20 (Roy. 14 E VI, f.110), 32 (Cotton Augustus I, i f.83), 59 (Add. MS 24098, f.21b), 62 (Add. MS 18855, f.108v), 70 (Cotton Augustus A v, f.124), 71 (Add. MS 19720, f.272v), 76 (Add. MS 18851, f.477v), 78 (MS Roy. 19c VIII f.41), 85 (from Jacopo de' Barbari, *Plan of Venice*), 87 (Add. MS 19720, f.305r), 98 (Add. MS 18851, f.2v); Bodleian Library, Oxford: 21 (MS Wood 276b, f.43v), 66 (Douce 219, f.153r), 94, 95 (MS Add. A46, f.1 to f.6r), 128 (MS Bodley 264, f.258); Christie's: 54 (School of Dieric Bouts, *Madonna and Child*), 15 (Master of The Legend of St Catherine, *Madonna and Child*, central panel of a triptych); Friedlander Archives: 100 (follower of Van der Weyden, *Virgin and Child*); M. Game: 107 B; Giraudon: 105 (Musée des Arts decoratifs, Paris, detail of tapestry with the Duke and Duchess of Orléans); Glamorgan Gwent Archaeological Trust: 73; P.D.A. Harvey and Oxford University Press: 25, 32; Judges Postcards Ltd, Hastings: 107 T; Kent Archaeological Society: 36 (*Archaeologia Cantiana* VII, pl.I, p.197); S. Landsberg: 16, 30, 42, 44, 64, 83, 91 (redrawn), 92 (redrawn), 93, 97, 103, 109, 111, 115 T & B, 116 (redrawn), 117, 123, 126, 127, 133, 135, 137, back cover; Leeds Castle Trustees: 12; Metropolitan Museum of Art, New York: 55 (*The Hunt of the Unicorn*, VII - Gift of John D. Rockefeller, Jr., The Cloisters Collection, 1937, 37.80.6); 88 (The Cloisters Collection, 1925, 25.120.227); Museu Nacional de Arte, Antigua, Lisbon: 14 (*Mystical Marriage of St Catherine*); Österreichische Nationalbibliothek, Vienna: front cover (Cod. 2617, f.53); H. Palmer: 2; C. Philo and the Wharram Research Project: 45; The Pierpont Morgan Library, New York: 27 (MS 399, f.3v); Royal Commission on the Historical Monuments of England, © Crown Copyright: 9; St Gallen, Stiftsbibliothek: 38 (Cod. 1092); Sotheby's, London, © 1972: 118; Sotheby's Inc., New York, © 1982: 22 (Master of the Embroidered Foliage, *The Virgin and Child*); C.C. Taylor: 24; Trinity College, Cambridge, Master and Fellows: 35 (MS R 17 1); Warburg Institute: 23, 52 (by the Master of the Love Garden); C. Webb: 82; E. Whittle: 122; Wiltshire Records Office: 45, 47 (Wilton Estate, *Survey of Lands of 1st Earl of Pembroke*, 2057 SB).

General Index

Numbers in italics refer to illustrations.

© 1995 Sylvia Landsberg

Published by British Museum Press
A division of The British Museum Company Ltd
46 Bloomsbury Street
London WC1B 3QQ

Sylvia Landsberg has asserted her right to be identified as the author of this work

ISBN 0- 7141- 2082- 4

A catalogue record for this book is available from the British Library

Designed and typeset by Roger Davies, CM3 1HT UK
Printed in Italy by Imago Publishing Ltd